The Bigger Picture

Elaine K Collier

ISBN 13: 978-1-7367389-3-1
Printed in the United States of America
First Printing, 2021

Journey Written ® Book-Writing & Publishing
Visit our website at www.JourneyWritten.com

Dedication

For June, without whose draft idea
my journey would never have begun.

Until the next time xx

Table of Contents

In the Beginning

"Let's go to the Spiritualist Church on Sunday," she said.

"Whatever for?" I asked.

"Dunno really, something to do."

And that was that.

June was my best friend. I say 'was' not because we fell out or anything but because she's passed now. We met when working together at a local firm of accountants in St Ives, Cambridgeshire, and our friendship was born. We had a lot in common, we were both born in London, the same age (well, actually, she was two years older and always claimed senior status) and shared the same warped sense of humour.

Constantly on the lookout for new and interesting things to do to relieve the boredom of an accountant's office, we had toyed with many new activities over the years. We took up keep fit, badminton, dancing, hairdressing, and even horse riding. All had their good points and all had us (and everyone around us) in fits of laughter, mainly because we were useless and loved to laugh far more than we loved what we were supposed to be doing.

So, the Spiritualist Church idea was, I thought, just another thing to try and tick off the list. Yes ok it was a bit unusual and I was sure that laughing might be frowned upon, but hell – why not! This would soon die a death and we would move on to our next great adventure.

I asked June what the point of going to the church was.

"To see if it exists, this life after death business," she replied, and I must admit that piqued my interest greatly. To be honest, I wasn't sure. My Mum had always told me that my granddad was in heaven and watching over me. I loved the thought of that and it gave me a lot of comfort, but as I grew older I began to wonder. Could the dead really go somewhere else? Surely once you died, that was it – after all the body was either buried or burnt, you weren't going anywhere from that!

So, the church it was and off we went one Sunday evening, full of apprehension.

"When we get in there," June said, "tell them nothing."

"What?"

"We don't want them remembering stuff about us which they can use later," she replied.

St Ives Spiritualist Church was basically just a couple of rooms in a big old building located down the dark and gloomy Free Church Passage. The big green door was not particularly welcoming, but in we went. The flight of stairs immediately in front was even more dark, gloomy and imposing than the front of the building. The whole place had a "feel" about it and I was getting a bit spooked.

"What's that smell?" I asked.

"Embalming fluid," she said.

"Jesus, how the bleeding hell do you know what embalming fluid smells like?"

"I don't, I'm just saying! And stop swearing, we're in a church!"

She was a fine one to talk, her language could match any navvy on a building site.

We opened the door to the right. Well, she did because I pushed her in first – after all she was the senior one! It was surprisingly bright, filled with rows of chairs and some sort of stage with a lectern at the front of the room. Not too many people but then we were early, 'to get a good seat' she claimed. For God's sake!

A woman came over and said *hello*, she had a nice smile and was welcoming. We sat down and waited.

Nothing much happened – what a let-down! I had envisioned all sorts of weird and wonderful things happening in that room that night – people levitating, chairs moving about on their own, people wailing and going into some sort of trance-like state, and so on. I mean, I had read about these types of things and people getting you hooked into their cult as soon as look at you!

But no, nothing like that at all. We sang hymns!

The highlight came towards the end of the evening when the Medium of the week started delivering messages from 'the other side'. Now this is what we came to see, this was going to be our proof of life after death one way or another but, to be honest, I wasn't sure whether I wanted a message or not.

I needn't have worried – no message! Nothing, nada, diddly bloody squat!

"Well, that was a waste of time," I said to June as we left the Church, "what do we do now?"

"We come back next week", she replied.

Life After Death?

My thoughts about life after death at that time were really that I had no bloody idea. I was young, just 29-years-old, so to be honest I didn't give death an awful lot of thought. After all, I was young and had many, many years ahead of me; I was still in that 'I'm invincible' stage. Like many, I had lost a few people close to me and although I grieved, I still didn't think too much about what happened after they died. That was until I lost my baby.

My granddad died when I was around 3 years old and mum told me he had gone to heaven to be with the Angels, but would always watch over me. So, from that age I suppose I sort of thought that death was simply going to another place.

My nan died when I was about 14 but although I was upset, she was old and had breast cancer. We had moved away from the area a few years earlier so I didn't see her that often so it wasn't such an impact on my daily life. I felt sad when I thought about her but, to be honest, that wasn't too often during my teenage years.

I remember when I was in my late teens a boy I knew quite well was killed in a motor bike accident and I found that tough. I had a hard time accepting that I would never see him again, there he was one minute and gone the next. He wasn't old, wasn't ill, and to my mind it wasn't supposed to happen. I didn't really understand then that your time was your time, no matter how old you were. It was a bit like having a sell-by date!

My biggest loss was when my mum died. I had just turned 18 and still lived at home, so not having her in my life anymore was major. Dad took me to the Chapel of Rest on the day of her funeral to say my final goodbyes. That was the first time I had ever seen a dead body. She looked peaceful after she had been ill for a long time, but she looked like she was sleeping and I just wanted to wake her up. I remember calling her but not a flicker. I grieved for a long time. The final picture of her body remains with me.

I used to talk to mum a lot after she had gone. I remember when I first found out that I was pregnant. I sat at the top of the stairs crying tears of joy and saying something along the lines of "Oh mum, I've only gone and done it! What do I do now?" Little did I know then that into the 8th month of my pregnancy, I was to lose my son.

It was at that point that I started to think more about life after death and whether it existed or not. It was hard for me to accept that when someone died they were gone and that was it. I could just about accept that the body had gone but what about the person, the personality, the essence that makes you, you? Surely that can't just be wiped out.

I began to hope that my baby, although he never lived in this world, had gone to heaven and was with granddad and the Angels. And if granddad was there, then surely mum had to be there too. And even though my baby hadn't lived, he would still have a little personality too, wouldn't he?

So many questions that I wanted answers to and now that I had been to the Spiritualist Church perhaps I could start to get some of those questions answered.

There is no death, only a change of worlds

Chief Seattle

June's Message

We went back to the Church week after week after week. In fact, so many weeks I lost count.

When she said, "we'll come back next week," I thought she meant for one week only. No – she meant we come back each week until one of us gets a message.

It took quite a while, much to my surprise, before that message came. In my own little mind, I thought that whoever was to give us a message would know we were there and would be rushing in to speak to us. Oh, how naïve could you be?

Finally, the night arrived for a message to be delivered, and it came to June. I don't know if I was annoyed or relieved, to be honest. I wanted a message, but I also dreaded it. I had heard so many messages from so many different mediums over the past weeks to realise that some were better than others. Some messages were so vague that they could be from anyone. I mean, when you're in your 80s and someone says: "I've got your Mother here" they're not likely to be wrong, are they? I wanted a message yes, but I wanted it to be so clear that it was obvious it came from spirit. Was that too much to ask?

Anyway, June got her message and although a lot of it was vague, there were some specific details. The medium kept going on about an old man wearing a flat cap, an old tweed-type jacket, and bicycle clips but didn't have a bike. This man apparently had popped in to say hello, and he was pleased to see her there. June couldn't relate to any of it, but the medium asked her to just hold onto it as she couldn't take it back or change it in any way.

We left the church that night totally disappointed. That's that then, I thought. Life after death probably does not exist and Junie's message was just a load of rubbish. I felt strangely bereft. I never went to the church with high expectations in the first place, but now I felt a sense of loss; what was that all about?

I'd been home for about an hour and June phoned.

"It's all true," she shouted down the phone. "I've just phoned Mum and that bloke was her brother and he always wore bike clips because he kept ferrets."

Bloody hell!

"That's all brilliant," I said, and I began to feel quite excited. "Now what do we do?"

"Well nothing," she replied, "we got what we went for. We got a message and now we know that there really is life after death. We don't have to go there anymore."

"Hang on," I said, "that was your message, not mine. I want a message." I said, like a petulant child.

"Ok, then we keep going until you get your message and then that's it. Is that ok?" she asked.

We went back the following week.

Messages from Spirit

So, these people from the church seemed to be saying that when you die the body dies and eventually ceases to be. But the essence that is you, your spirit or your soul, lives on and goes to heaven. Hmmmm, that's just about what I had thought, but how do I know that's true? Well, this is where the mediums come into play.

The mediums claim that they can talk to the spirits of dead people.

Well, ok but how do they do that then? I learned that there were two types of medium – the natural ones who had the gift of communicating with the dead from birth, and those who train to become a medium. They tune in to a different frequency, much like turning the dial on a radio, and hey presto – a connection is made.

But what about some of the crap messages I've heard given out? What about those mediums that roll out what seemed to be stock phrases like "I've got your mother here" when the recipient is 90 herself, "and she sends you her love and says she's well". Oh, come on, pleeeease. Of course, that's what the recipient wants to hear, we all want to know that our loved ones are safe and well and they still love us.

So, is mediumship just capitalising on people's grief? Well, in some cases that might be so, but at the spiritualist churches the mediums usually only get paid travel expenses. They are people who turn out week after week in all weathers to deliver messages from the dead for little or no reward. Would you want to do that? I know I wouldn't.

Over many years, I've come to understand that being a medium is bloody hard work. In most cases, they didn't choose to become mediums, they were drawn to it. In fact, when you decide to work for spirit you don't always get to choose what you want to do but are drawn and sometimes pushed, often kicking and screaming, towards what is meant for you – your purpose as it were.

I never chose any of the work that I did for spirit, but I knew at the time what was right for me. I can't really explain how I knew, gut instinct and intuition I guess, but over the years I've discovered that if something is meant for me then it flows well, but if it isn't then I struggle and nothing really works out the way I want it to.

So, going back to talking to dead people – yes you really can! I've done it myself. But I know I wouldn't like to be a medium. They work hard in developing their skills and I get extremely upset when they are portrayed on TV as fakes and charlatans.

Some people need the reassurance that a medium can give, that their loved ones are indeed safe, well and free from pain. If they're going to a spiritualist church they're not being exploited or ripped off. There is no fee for the mediums' services unless you want a private reading. Like any church it's individual choice if, and how much, you donate to the collection box.

I used to love going to the spiritualist church and listening to the messages, but for me it was the hook that got me delving deeper into spirituality.

My Message

And so, we went back. Week after bloody week, waiting and wondering when my message would come.

Over the months, I really began to enjoy going to the Church every Sunday evening. The people were nice and friendly, not trying to join us up to some cult, and I was learning stuff that I had no idea about. I mean, who knew that you could potentially heal someone through your hands!

This was becoming a new way of life for me, and I looked forward to Sundays.

My message eventually came and when it did it completely blew me away.

The medium of the evening was a lovely lady and I was drawn to her from the beginning. You know, those types of people that you feel some sort of connection with, even though you've never met them before. When my turn came, she looked at me for a while before she spoke. I felt a little unsettled, what on earth was she going to say?

"You look too young, but I have your Mother here with me." Well yes, my mother had died when I was just 18, 11-years earlier. I could totally accept that and I felt chills up my arms.

And then it came.

"She's holding a baby. This is not the baby that you're expecting now but a child that has passed." I was totally floored by that. I was indeed pregnant at the time but only just. June was the only person who knew, except my husband of course. The baby she was holding was the child I had lost 2-years previously. She told me that Mum was saying my lost baby was safe and well and surrounded by love.

The medium went on to tell me other things, but the main message was that I wasn't to worry as my pregnancy would be fine and my baby delivered safely. She even told me that if I was knitting then to use blue wool! I was in floods of tears and so was June. We clung to each other, in total shock that the message I had just received was so spot on and that my Mum had my lost baby.

We left the church that evening in a total daze.

"Now what?" June asked.

"Well we have to continue," I replied. "We now know that there is life after death, but there's more to all of this than just that. We can't stop now, we just can't."

I don't know where I'm going, but I'm on my way.

Carl Sagan

Life After Death

Once I had received that message I was totally convinced that there was indeed life after death. I mean, how on earth did that medium know those things about me? Nobody in the church knew that I was pregnant let alone about the baby that I had lost. And how did she know about Mum, I was only 29 years old so my mum should still have been alive.

As you know by now, Mum had always told me that when Granddad died he'd gone to heaven to be with the Angels and would always be watching over me. I didn't doubt her for a minute. Well, I was a child and believed everything she told me, so going to another place when you died was sort of normal to me. I had the full expectation of going to this special place too, once I was old enough to die, and Granddad would be there and he would look after me.

This medium had just confirmed that there was indeed another place and Granddad, Mum and my baby were already there.

Of course, I had no idea what this special place was like. I once worked with a girl who told me that when you died you went to heaven and sat around on clouds all day eating peas! Oh, for God's sake, that was just plain bloody stupid. In my mind, I made heaven somewhere lovely, a bit like a luxury holiday destination. Heaven on Earth eh?

I wondered whether we would keep our same bodies when we went to Heaven, which would be a bit of a shame really as I didn't particularly like mine and I would love to swap it for a better model. I wondered what people did all day, not eat peas that was for sure. But did they go to work, go out with friends, and so on.

I wondered what they did eat. I hoped they had nice food. I had been to the States a few years previously to visit my husband's family and had tried my first MacDonald's and oh how I loved it. This was long before MacDonald's became popular here in the UK, so I rather hoped that there would be an unlimited supply in heaven.

I wondered if they lived with their families, because if they did surely that would cause a bit of a problem with second marriages?

Oh, I wondered about so many things and I didn't have a clue about any of this life after death business. There was so much I needed to learn.

It was about this time that I started reading books by Doris Stokes. For those who have not heard of her, Doris was a spiritual medium who came to fame through her books, TV shows and live performances. I read her first book, *Voices in My Ear*, and became hooked. She had lost a child too so I felt we had a bond. I think over the years I read most, if not all, of her books and they answered a lot of my questions. Of course, that was just the tip of the iceberg but it was a start. There was so much more than I ever realised and I never thought that this was just the start of my lifelong spiritual quest.

I went on to read many books by many different authors over the years, but I will always be grateful to Doris Stokes for raising more questions than she alone could answer.

Healing & Circle Work

We didn't stop going to church. June agreed that there was much more to learn and so we went back nearly every Sunday for around 5 years. It was an amazing time for both of us.

I was learning that there was so much more to spirituality than just getting messages from Spirit every Sunday evening, as nice as that was. But the messages were just evidence really that there is life after death. If the spirit lived on, then I wanted to know where they went and what they did when they got there.

Some people thrive on the comfort that the messages from their loved ones give them, and that's all they really go to the church for. And that's perfectly ok. Others who are grieving seek out mediums to give them reassurance that their loved ones have indeed gone to a better place. It's these people I do worry about that at a vulnerable phase they could be totally duped by unscrupulous people and, of course, it's the charlatans that are always portrayed in the media and on TV. If you feel the need for a medium then please do your homework first, go on positive recommendations or go to a church.

Thursday night was "healing" night in the Church. People would pop in for some healing for all sorts of things and members of the Church would administer. Curious, I asked if I could go along to better understand the process.

"Yes, of course," one of the ladies replied, "and we can start to show you how to work with healing."

Blimey! Hadn't expected that but I was so willing to have a go. Their healing was simple, they just placed hands on the person being healed and asked Spirit to assist. Bloody hell, if it was that easy to heal people why weren't more people doing it and why was there so much sickness in the world, and why wasn't our medical profession using it? I had so many questions.

Later I learned that intent was everything. What we focused on was crucial to the outcome.

I was amazed by those healing sessions. My body grew hot and my fingers swelled – it felt like I had big fat sausages on the ends of my hands. Not only that, I was beginning to feel some of the symptoms that my 'patients' were feeling. Those who came for healing walked away feeling much better than when they came in. It was an amazing feeling to know that you have helped someone in some way, but I was warned not to let ego take over as this had nothing to do with me, I was merely the channel through which the healing energy could flow.

I was to learn a lot about healing in the years that followed but at that time I thought I knew it all – yeah, well, I was young.

One of the things that June and I really wanted to get into was circle work. Circle work is when a group of people sit together, in a circle, with the specific purpose of contacting spirit. This isn't to get messages from loved ones, more to learn about what happens when we die and spirituality in general. Our church, at that time, was run by mainly older people and was very traditional. Their views went along the lines of you had to be a member of the church for eleven billion years before you could even be considered for circle work.

However, we could attend the Open Circle once a month if we wished.

The Open Circle was different from Closed Circles. In the open one anyone could go but it was mainly to help individuals to develop their mediumship and connection skills. The Closed Circle however was for a smaller group of people who agreed on, and sat for, a specific purpose.

We were both very disappointed – how were we supposed to learn and progress if we couldn't participate in such things. Getting messages from the dead was all very well, but we both had this need to know more and to discover what life was all about. Why were we here in the first place? But we grabbed the opportunity of the monthly Open Circle and it was certainly a great learning opportunity. We learnt a lot about circle work and after a year or so we felt confident enough to start our own private circle.

Oh, how this was frowned upon but by this time we had made it to President and Secretary (mainly because no one else wanted the job!) and we had the keys to the church! Now we were very naïve in those days and impatient to get started. We found another young couple who were just as eager and, ignoring all the sound advice about having someone who knows what they are doing present, we started our Circle.

We hadn't got a bloody clue about running a circle, but we had sat in the open circles and read a few books so thought we'd be ok. We went along with what we thought was instinct, but I know now that we were guided. We knew that we had to sit with love, pure thoughts and intentions and we had to protect ourselves.

So, there we were on Tuesday evenings, just four of us in the Church. Strange how spooky it felt with just us there, especially when we turned the lights off and just had the dim altar lights on. We sat, me opposite June and the couple opposite each other. We had absolutely no idea what to do, but knew that we had to ask for protection from our guides, sit with love and light, and build up the energy.

June led the circle, well she would, being the oldest! She opened with a prayer and told us to start building energy by imagining a glowing disc of orange in the centre of the circle at about waist level. We did that for about an hour and guess what – nothing happened, although I'm sure if anything had happened we would have all shit ourselves. Disappointed or what? I thought this would be easy.

We kept trying, week after week we grew that orange glowing disc. Progress was slow. One week I started to feel a familiar pulling behind the eyes, just like I had when I was a child in my bedroom. I also felt sick, physically sick, it could have been something dodgy I had eaten but I didn't like it. But it happened the following week and the week after that. I felt so sick some nights that I thought I would have to go out and throw up. I didn't like it, I mean who does like that feeling of about to throw up?

After a few weeks the nausea passed, but nothing more was happening. Still we sat. Then one night, totally out of the blue, we made a breakthrough.

"Oh," I said, "it feels like something has just bashed into my left side." It was quite a significant bash and I felt like it had caused me to bend over to the right.

"Okay," said June, "now don't be alarmed but I can see an open door on your left side and it was the door swinging open that crashed into you. There's a flight of stairs and a man at the top with his arm out, stopping people coming down the stairs. Behind him there are loads of people all waving at us and shouting out hello."

Shitting bloody hell, what was that all about?

But that was it for that night, and for several weeks after that. Blimey, spirit works so slowly doesn't it?

We continued and we grew. As the weeks passed, more and more happened. We learnt that the guy at the top of the stairs was our Gatekeeper and he would only let through those who needed to be let through.

We always worked in the same way. I would physically feel spirit, could feel pressure on my body, and I just seemed to know things without knowing how I knew them, if that makes sense. I later learned that this was a mix of *clairsentience* which loosely translated means "clear-feeling", and *claircognizance* which means "clear-knowing". There are other "clairs", the best-known being *clairvoyance*, or "clear-seeing".

So, whilst I knew when spirit was drawing near and could pick up on their thoughts and feelings and just knew why they were with us, June complimented that by seeing what I was feeling. The other two in the group added detail.

We worked well as a team and we went from strength to strength. We learnt how to work with spirit, how to protect ourselves and our circle, and learnt that we could say no to spirit if we didn't feel easy or comfortable with them. We learnt that we had guides working with us, both individually and guides who came to teach us.

I learnt to say the first things that came into my head without trying to analyse them and without allowing my own thoughts to get in the way. I think this was one of the most valuable lessons I learned, to simply get out of my own way, stop doubting what I was getting and allowing spirit to come through unhindered.

We eventually had a spell as a rescue circle, sending lost souls into the light. This was highly rewarding but also very draining.

We met our guides and those who would work with us in our spiritual development.

I remember one night we met a guide that June and I shared. He came to me with something quite heavy on his head and something large placed around his neck, shoulders and chest. He came with so much love for both of us and I was feeling quite choked emotionally. When June eventually saw him, she described a tallish gold hat type thing on his head and around the shoulders was a white-ish leather type collar engraved with golden hieroglyphics. He was of the Aztec type people, but not an Aztec. Apparently in a past life I was his wife and June was our child.

Oh, for God's sake, really? That really did cause quite a stir and sent us into fits of laughter – it took a long while to stop her calling me Mum!

Seriously though, it was no wonder that we felt such a deep connection and formed a deep friendship from the moment we met. Have you ever felt that immediate connection with someone you have just met? You know you know them, but probably not from this lifetime.

The main lesson we learned from those early days of circle work was never give up trying. We kept on and on, even during the weeks and months that nothing happened. Eventually we succeeded and boy, it was simply amazing when we did.

The overall feeling for me at that time was a great sense of familiarity and being exactly where I should be. Something that had been previously missing was now firmly in my life.

Spiritual Work

I never realised that when we started to sit in a circle that we were, in fact, working for spirit. It was just something that intrigued us and was the next step in finding out more about spirituality.

I didn't think that ordinary people like me, or June, could work for spirit, I thought you had to be special in some way. After all, we were both as down to earth as they came, we loved life and having a good time, we liked a party and having a drink or three, we swore a lot, but we had kind hearts and were always there for those who needed a bit of help. I remember Junie's Mum used to say that people like us were the salt of the earth – whatever that meant!

The few spiritual people that I knew or had read about seemed different in some way. It was as if there was a certain air about them, they held such knowledge that somehow made them special and above the rest of us. Those were the people I aspired to be like, I wanted to be special too, not just plain old salt of the earth me!

Years later I came to understand that we're all special in our own way and that is exactly as it should be. My being totally down to earth in no way prevented me from being spiritual, in fact it helped draw other down to earth people to me who had a quest for more spiritual knowledge.

The circle work taught me a lot. I learned that we all have spiritual guides who work with us throughout this lifetime. Some are with us as we come into this world and they will be with us when we leave. Other guides come and go as we move through our lives. They're here to help, guide and teach us.

My first guide who made himself known to me was a Native American Indian called Blue Hawk. I wasn't aware of him until I was told of his presence by a member of our church. He taught me a lot about nature and healing. He taught me how to respect all aspects of nature and how it was our life support system. He's not with me much these days, but quite often comes when I meditate outside.

My next guide, who is still with me today, made himself known to me by giving me the feeling that someone was poking their finger in my right ear. Yeah, I know, only I could have a guide who stuck a finger in my ear. For some strange reason, I called him Mr Wilson. He comes to help me with life issues, and when the going gets tough I can rely on him to talk some sense into me. He is a no-nonsense kind of guy so there's not much frivolity when he comes but I love him anyway and I am grateful to have him with me.

I remember once, many years ago now, when my son was on a school trip to France. Late one evening I had a phone call to say that Jordan was unwell, he had a raging temperature and his teachers were concerned enough to call the doctor. At that time, they didn't know what was wrong but would call me the following morning after the doctor's visit. I was all for jumping on a plane there and then but Pat talked sense and suggested we wait until the following morning when I would have more news. Needless to say, it was a sleepless night but I do remember that at one point Mr Wilson was with me. My mind talk went something like this:

Mr Wilson: "Stay calm, all will be well."

Me: "It's ok for you to say but it's not your child."

Mr Wilson: "You are all my children, we're all connected. He will be fine."

Me: "It's meningitis, isn't it?"

Mr Wilson: "No, he has an ear infection, all will be well."

Me: "How can you be sure? We're still waiting for the doctor."

Mr Wilson: "Trust me."

Early the following morning I had a phone call from France. The doctor had been, Jordan had an ear infection and had been prescribed antibiotics.

Many years later, whilst in a Spiritual Development Workshop, I was told that Mr Wilson was elderly and hard of hearing so he used an ear trumpet and yes, it was in his right ear. He was a teacher and had a stern and 'proper' disposition. It all started to make perfect sense to me then, the feelings I had matched the person he was.

Blimey, who would have thought it eh? Not only did I have these guides working with me but I could communicate with them and, it seemed, accurately.

Religion is belief in someone else's experience, spirituality is having your own experience.
Deepak Chopra

Moorfields Eye Hospital

Let me tell you a bit more about the weird pulling sensation behind the eyes that I felt in the early days of our circle work. It was as if I was being drawn into something or a place that I didn't know. I'd had that feeling as a child but now it began to make sense.

When I was young, I had the bedroom that used to belong to my Granddad and for some reason one of his pictures still hung on the wall. I can't remember it too clearly, it was either Jesus or Mary and made from coloured foil so it had a beautiful iridescence to it.

Anyway, when I was around 7 years old this picture used to draw me into it. Night after night, when I closed my eyes to go to sleep I felt this strangest feeling of being drawn into the picture and this drawing feeling seemed to be coming from behind my eyes. I fought it, I didn't want to go, it scared me.

Eventually I told my mum because it got to the point where I was scared to go to bed each night. In my child's mind, I thought there was someone living behind the picture who was trying to take me off somewhere.

Mum thought it might be a physical problem with my eyes! Why on earth she would think that I have no idea but I guess to her it was logical. She took me to the doctor. He couldn't see anything immediately wrong but sent me to the eye hospital, just to be sure.

Off we went to Moorfields Eye Hospital. They couldn't see anything obvious either but just to be on the safe side they gave

Mum some drops to put in my eyes and made another appointment for the following week.

Mum dutifully put the drops in my eyes. I couldn't see a thing when they went in and spent the following week fumbling my way around school. It was horrible and I was convinced I was going blind. Mum and Dad thought I was going blind too. That went on for a week!

Back we went to Moorfields. They looked in my eyes again with those big horrible machines. It didn't hurt but there was a lot of light.

There was a lot of adult conversation about me. It seemed they couldn't find anything wrong with my eyes at all which was a huge relief, especially as we all thought I was going blind.

But it turned out that Mum had been putting those drops into my eyes for a whole week when they only needed to go in on the morning of the appointment!

We went home, no more drops and my eyesight returned to normal. No, I wasn't going blind, and there was nothing wrong with my eyes.

That strange feeling at night stopped just after that, until that night in a circle.

Spirit and Children

Now I know more about the spirit world, it's all perfectly clear what was happening at that time.

Children have the natural ability to connect with spirit readily and easily up to the age of about seven. They are open channels because they have retained that memory of coming from spirit, it is their natural state.

How many stories have you heard about imaginary friends? Your own children may have had them, or friends' children, you may have even had one yourself. Children can have great long dialogues with them, and can even describe them in detail. But how do you know what that child is seeing and experiencing? Simple – you don't. You can't see it so therefore it doesn't exist.

Around the age of seven those imaginary friends start to disappear. Why? Because parents, family, society starts to tell children that their friends are all in their head, are not real, they don't exist.

Why do we do that? Because society has already shaped us into believing that what we can't see doesn't exist. We see only what's in our own reality. It's only the curious and open-minded that accepts that anything is possible until it's proven otherwise. It wasn't until explorers provided evidence of never falling off the end of the world that people started to accept that it wasn't flat.

But stop and think for a moment. We can't see radio frequencies but we know they exist. We know they exist because when we turn the dial on a radio we can tune into whatever station we choose.

It's the same with spirit. They exist on a different frequency. Children have the natural ability to turn that dial and tune into the frequency where their 'imaginary friend' exists. When the child is constantly told it's all in their heads, they stop turning the dial. Isn't that sad?

Rescue Circle Work

We continued to sit in circle for years, much to the annoyance of some of the older members of the church. Eventually we turned into a Rescue Circle although we had no idea that's what it was until someone explained it to us. Apparently, we were attracting restless souls, those who had passed but had no idea where they were or what had happened to them. Some didn't even realise they were dead and this often happened during a sudden death. They were trapped between two worlds, living closer to the earth plain than the spiritual. Can you imagine how frightening that must be? They were drawn towards our light and energy that we were sending out from the circle and it was our job to point them in the right direction and help them to move onwards.

Sometimes it could be quite harrowing work especially when, as a group, we often experienced how that person died and the circumstances surrounding it.

I could never, and still can't, see spirit but I could sense them close to me. I could feel what they felt, both physically and emotionally. June could see and describe in detail what she was seeing. The other two in the circle filled in the gaps, so between the four of us we had a complete picture.

Some of these poor souls suffered horribly and most of the cases we dealt with were usually because of accident or murder.

Some nights it took ages to help an individual and we would not leave until we knew that a soul had moved onwards to the place where they needed to be. In my experience, I've never encountered a soul who didn't want to be helped. It was as if they knew they were lost and just needed that little bit of a nudge and guidance to move onwards.

It became very clear to me at that time that when people claim places are haunted, it is in fact just these lost souls who have no idea of what has happened to them and are clinging to what they know, their homes and their loved ones. Sometimes they have been doing this for hundreds of years, but remember that's hundreds of years in our time, in our reality. In the spirit world, there is no time!

It was such rewarding work but we had to be very careful that we closed our circle down completely and disconnected ourselves so as not to take away the more negative aspects of the work we did. I never had a problem personally, I could completely detach once the circle had closed, but I do know that some people find it difficult to draw the line between the spiritual work they do and the world in which they live.

Church Officers
& Spiritual Writing

June and I continued being active members in our Church, and in circle, for several years. Eventually, as it always did, the time came around once again to elect a new president and committee and, typical of all committees, no one was interested!

"We could do it", June said to me one day.

"Are you mad?" I replied.

"No," she said, "I've thought about this overnight and I could be the President and you could be the Secretary."

Sodding hell, she had seriously lost the plot this time. Of all her madcap ideas this one had to be the worst. I mean, for heaven's sake what did we know about running a Spiritualist Church. The idea was simply insane! Never going to happen.

And so, it was that just a few weeks later we found ourselves wholeheartedly elected as the new President and Secretary of St Ives Spiritualist Church. I would like to think it was because the members liked us and thought we were good enough to do the job, but it's more likely that no-one else wanted to take it on.

It was typical of June wanting to become President: she loved to swan about and be the centre of attention. That's not a criticism of her, it's simply the way she was and I loved her dearly. My role was a bit more involved and one of my tasks was to book the weekly mediums. Here was my chance to bring in some good ones, keep the popular ones we already had and clear out some of the dross.

We were also responsible for running the Sunday service each week. One of us would oversee proceedings, give an address and introduce the Medium of the week. All straightforward, but we did have to come up with something to talk about during our short address.

I do have to admit to being a bit of a procrastinator, I will always put stuff off to the last minute! On weeks when it was my turn to take the service I would go up to my bedroom about 4pm and start to plan what I was going to say. More often than not, my mind would go blank and I'd go into panic as yet again I'd left it to the last minute and had nothing to say. In the end, I'd ask my spirit guides to inspire me. And inspire me they did.

Once I had pen and paper at the ready the words would just flow. I'm still not quite sure how it all worked but words came into my mind and I just allowed them to flow onto the paper, without thinking or correcting them in any way. It was only when the words stopped flowing that I would read it all back and make sense of it.

I'll share with you a poem that flowed one week but before I do I just want to say that although I was a member and indeed the Secretary of the church, I certainly didn't understand the workings of spirit very much at all. I only went to the church in the first place to try to prove to myself that there was some form of life after death and I had achieved that. However, in answering one question umpteen more took its place. I came to understand that there was much more to spirituality than just knowing we continued to exist long after our physical body had died. And so I questioned and I still question to this very day. But questioning is good, it's the way we learn.

At this time, I was questioning why there was so much horrible stuff going on in the world, especially where children were concerned, and why people were so horrible to each other. This is what came back:

Do not judge others too harshly
My Guide said to me last week
Give them your love and compassion
You know nothing of their tasks to meet

We should give them care and understanding
And try to help them through this life
Send out our prayers to all of them
That their next lesson is free from strife.

We should give them our admiration
They've chosen this pathway to take
And while many paths are much simpler
Theirs's a much harder choice to make

Yet it's hard to give love and compassion
When a man causes a child to cry
And it's hard to give care and understanding
When a man causes a child to die

It's impossible to give admiration
To men who commits these crimes
What pleasure do they gain from it?
I ask, so many times.

So I'm trying to be very spiritual
But I live in a material world
And while part of me does understand
I still can't help being repelled.

So I will continue to battle
With two different parts of me
To bring my material and spiritual
Into much greater harmony.

I'll pray for all of the children
Who suffer at somebody's hands
That when it's their time to pass over
They will finally understand

Changing Jobs

And so, life continued for a good few years. My son, Jordan, was born not too long after we started going to the church. We had a naming ceremony for him a couple of years later. A lovely medium, Dennis Nelson, officiated. Jordan was blessed and given his spirit name. It was a lovely Sunday afternoon and we were surrounded by friends and family. Jordan wasn't too impressed however, all he wanted to do was play the organ. But, nevertheless, I felt that spirit had welcomed him although I know that we didn't have to do the ceremony for that to happen.

I loved the church and my ever-growing spirituality. I still had a lot to learn but it felt as if I had found a part of me that had been missing.

June and I were pootling along with Church on Sunday and still coming up with mad schemes to make life sparkle more. If I thought joining a spiritualist church was a mad idea, her suggestion that we take up horse riding was possibly the most stupid.

I thought that's how our life would be from now onwards but no, the universe and spirit had other plans for us! In fact, I was told one evening during a healing session that I would leave the church and spirituality as I had a life to live but I would return some time in the future. *Pah, load of old rubbish,* I thought, I could never see me giving up the church and my spiritual quest.

But a big change was certainly in store for me. I had worked at a firm of Accountants since I left school and, to be honest, it was boring. No disrespect to accountants out there, if you love what you do then it's perfect for you. But I didn't. I fell into the job after my interview with the Careers Officer as I was due to leave school. Basically, I had two choices – I could either work in a bank or train to become a nurse. I chose the bank because I didn't see myself as a nurse, to be honest. The thought of messing about with sick people wasn't my dream job but then neither was a bank to be fair! I honestly didn't know what I wanted to do and at 16 I don't think many people do. This was in the late 1960s and girls especially didn't have the choices that are available to them now. University just didn't come onto the agenda – my parents certainly couldn't afford it and I just didn't want to go. I was too busy having a good social life with my mates at home.

So, the Accountants it was. I started as an office junior and earned £8 a week! Life wasn't all dull and we had some laughs, but the work was repetitive and boring. Then June joined the firm and injected some much-needed sparkle.

I remember one day, I was standing talking to one of our older members of staff, Ada, in her office. It was a hot day and she had the window open at the bottom. Suddenly something was being lowered from the office window above. I couldn't believe my eyes and found it so hard not to burst out laughing. Ada had bought a chicken from the shop during her lunch break but because the weather was hot and her office stuffy, she had placed it on a plate on her windowsill to keep cool. One of the boys had been into the office whilst Ada was out and took the chicken, and he and June were in the office above, had tied a string round one of its legs and were lowering down past Ada's window. She couldn't see it but I could. I could also hear their shrieks of laughter coming from the office above. I got out of there as fast as I could and flew up the stairs to rescue the chicken. I can reassure you that the chicken wasn't harmed in any way and June put it back on the windowsill as soon as she could. Ada never knew what an adventure her chicken had been on.

Junie had a larger-than-life character, she laughed a lot and was so much fun. She lived just around the corner and would catch the bus to work two stops after me. From the minute she plonked herself down we would start laughing, and by the time we got off in town the whole bus was laughing along with us. We used to do a lot of crazy things together but one of my favourites was catching the train to London to see some of her family and popping round the Pie & Mash shop. If you were born and raised in London, especially around the East End, then you will know the draw of Pie & Mash.

One morning, during our coffee break at work, I was feeling more bored and fed-up than usual, and I started scanning through the jobs section of our local paper. I didn't really have any intention of changing my job but just thought I'd have a look and see what was available in my small part of the world.

There was a vacancy for a Personnel Officer at a research institute just up the road from where I lived. Nowadays it's the much grander title of Human Resources Officer but back then it was simply Personnel! The advert didn't say too much but it sounded like the type of work I would like to do, very people based rather than just stuck in an office counting numbers. June peered over my shoulder.

"What's that then?" she asked.

I pointed to the advert and she agreed it could be interesting and why didn't I just give them a ring ask for further details.

"You've got nothing to lose," she said. "If you don't like the sound of it you don't have to do anything else."

She was right so I phoned and they said yes, they would pop the details in the post.

A couple of days later an envelope popped through my door with not only the further details but an application form as well.

As soon as June got on the bus that morning I waved the envelope at her.

"It's come," I said. She had a look and agreed with me that the job looked good.

"Why don't you apply?" she asked. "You probably won't get an interview so you've really got nothing to lose, have you?"

I filled in the application form and posted it before I could change my mind.

A few days later I got a letter inviting me to attend an interview.

"Bloody hell June," I said, as soon as she sat next to me on the morning bus to work, "I've only gone and got an interview. Now what?"

"Just go to the interview. You probably won't get the job so you've got nothing to lose, have you?"

I went to the interview on Wednesday morning. The more I found out about the job the more I liked it but, as Junie said, I probably wouldn't get the job so I didn't think too much about it.

On Friday evening, they phoned and offered me the job! They told me to think about it over the weekend but asked if I could give them my answer by Monday. Shit – now what? I phoned June.

"They've offered me the job," I screamed down the phone. "Now what do I do?"

"Ah well babe," she said, "you're on your own here, I can't tell you what to do."

Bloody hell, there she was one minute telling me that it probably wouldn't come to much and now I'd got the job she was backing out. All that makes me sound as if I don't have a mind of my own, doesn't it? But believe me, nothing could be further from the truth. I knew in my heart what I was going to do, I just needed my head to catch up.

I took the job!

Whatever you are not changing, you are choosing

Unknown

New Job, New Friends

The new job was everything I wanted it to be. It took a while to settle in and make new friends, but once I did I loved every minute of being at work.

The Administration Building was totally separate from the main buildings and the other staff and, overall, the admin staff tended to keep themselves to themselves. They were a nice bunch but mainly older than me and fun and laughter was in short supply.

The main building was a listed building and full of character, the grounds were amazing with lots of trees and plants and we even had a pond. There was a staff canteen with, would you believe, a swimming pool just in the front of it. There was a very active social club for those who were interested. Blimey, this was right up my street.

Not long after I joined, a new girl, Kate, started in the typing pool. We hit it off immediately and shared a lot of laughs together. In fact, one day we got told off for laughing so much. For God's sake is there a limit to the amount you should laugh in a day? I must say that the woman who told us off was very pinched and dry and had a face like a slapped arse. I shouldn't think she'd seen much excitement or a lot of fun in her life!

Kate and I used to go across to the canteen for lunch and slowly we began to make more friends.

The social life was amazing, with a very active Sports and Social Club. The canteen was used for all sorts of events and summer evenings were fabulous sitting around the swimming pool. Every day-time event always ended with a disco!

It was during a Quiz Night that I met Pat for the first time. I had seen her around but only just to say hello to. Kate and I were part of the Admin Quiz Team and after the quiz was over and the rest of Admin went home, we stayed on and had a few more drinks. Pat came over and introduced herself and another friendship was born. I didn't know then what a major role Pat would have in my life.

Pat, Kate and I did a lot of social stuff together, both inside and outside of work. We really hit it off and had a good time. Pat was on the Social Committee and she wrote and produced shows and pantomimes. These were always great fun and of course Kate and I were always involved. We had inter-departmental *It's a Knockout* competitions which were filled with good natured rivalry. We made more and more friends and my working life couldn't be better.

Pat and I, and our respective husbands, became great friends and formed a solid foursome. We socialised a lot and even took holidays together. They had no children, so they really spoiled Jordan and he loved all the attention he got. They became his second parents in a way, and he always knew where to go when he needed something.

I was really happy, life was good and I was so pleased I took the job.

Taking the Leap

I learnt from that whole experience that if you're not prepared to take a leap of faith sometimes you will never get anywhere. You must make change happen. I wasn't happy in my job, I was bored stupid and I felt stifled although I loved the people I worked with and I had some wonderful friends. We would often all go out socially and our annual day trips to London to see a show and have a meal were the highlights of the year.

We saved £1 a week in our little syndicate. It doesn't sound a lot but back then it paid for our theatre tickets, train fare with a little over for a couple of drinks. All we had to find was some money for food, and a few more drinks. We always did the day in style, catching the early morning train into London and then the last train back in the evening. One year will be forever etched in my memory – breakfast at the Dorchester, lunch in the Pie & Mash shop, tea at the Ritz and dinner at the Savoy. How on earth did we manage to eat so much food in one day? Not to mention the numerous bottles of wine we consumed as well. I can't remember what show we saw that year but I do remember we got on the wrong train home and the end of the line was in Stevenage! We had about an hour to wait before the next train so ended up in the pub by the station. Funny how every station has a pub close by. When we opened the door the smoke and the smell of cannabis hit us like a force field. It was about 10:30 at night and the pub was heaving with young people, it must have been well known as the local den of iniquity. We spent a very happy hour in there and by the time we finally got on the train we were all as high as kites.

Anyway, I digress from the point I'm trying to make here. By changing my job, I took a great leap of faith. The job might have been awful and I might have hated every minute of being there, but on the other hand it might not. I might not work with such a fabulous bunch of people or make friends, but on the other hand I might. When we take a leap we never know what we're really leaping to, but I knew that by staying in the same place nothing would ever change. If I wanted to change my life then I had to make it happen and I had been given a golden opportunity.

Many years later my son gave me a book.

"Read this Mum, I think you'll like it." It was *Big Magic* by Elizabeth Gilbert, and I enjoyed it so much that I read it from start to finish on a 7-hour flight to Dubai. One sentence really struck a chord with me. It was something along the lines of "opportunities float by us all the time and if we don't grab them as they pass they float on by to the next person who may very well grab them and turn them into something fabulous".

On the day, I accepted my new job I grabbed an opportunity as it floated by and in the years to come I would grab many more.

Opportunities don't come along often. So, when they do you have to grab them.

Audrey Hepburn

My Husband

I've not mentioned my husband at all have I? I married at 19, which was far too young and, if I'm being perfectly honest, was a total mistake. Looking back, I think I married to get away from home. It was the early 70's and living together was not as widely accepted as it is now. I knew my Dad would never approve.

My Mum had died a couple of years earlier at the age of 46 and I was devastated. I had already met Denis, my husband, at that time and when I lost Mum I turned to him more to help me through a difficult period. When he asked me to marry him I saw no reason not to.

Dad had started seeing someone else and although I liked her very much, she was not my Mum and I wasn't too happy with her being in my Mum's home. Selfish I know. I wanted Dad to be happy and so the easiest thing was for me to marry and move out of the family home.

Denis and I were married in June 1973 and moved into a flat not too far from Dad and the rest of my family. Life was pretty good to start with, although it was never the mad passionate love that you should have when you first marry. However, we poodled along together and rode some of the storms of life.

Nine years on and I became pregnant with our first child but sadly lost him in late pregnancy. I was devastated but a couple of years later I was pregnant again and this time I gave birth to a beautiful healthy baby boy – Jordan.

I loved being at home with my new baby, but we couldn't afford for me to stay home permanently so I went back to work. It was a few years later that I changed jobs.

Denis liked to remain very much within his comfort zone, which was basically work and home. He was not a social creature at all, whereas I was just the opposite. I loved people and I loved to party, his idea of going out was going over to his Mum's for a cup of tea. Denis came to a few social events with me but it was blatantly clear that he hated every moment of it. He would sit with his face on and eventually it was easier to give in and just go home. He also hated me going out with Junie or any other friends.

I remember one night just before Christmas. June and I had started an evening hairdressing course, another one of our mad but fun things to do. It was fun to be honest, because we laughed our way through the whole 6-weeks of it. On the last night, everyone went to the pub for a drink and as June and I had got a lift with someone else that night we had no choice but to go too. I'm not making excuses here, we both wanted to go very much. We didn't stay long, about an hour, and just had a couple of drinks but in that hour Denis and June's husband, also called Dennis, had decided we'd gone missing, something terrible must have happened to us and so they called the police!

Not only did Denis want to remain within his comfort zone, he wanted me to remain in it too. He had grown up in a home where both parents worked incredibly hard and didn't go out much at all. When his Dad wasn't at work he was tending his large garden, and growing enough fruit and veg to feed his family. His Mum not only had a full-time job but she ran the home too. She had three sons and did everything for them, I think she was probably too exhausted to have a social life too. Denis wanted to continue with the lifestyle he had grown up with and he expected me to fall into it too.

I, on the other hand, was raised by parents who enjoyed the company of others and had a good social life. Growing up I lived among extended family. My Dad had three siblings and his step-mum had around five children of her own. Nan lived two streets away from us and I remember the numerous family parties at her house. Always a good old-fashioned knees-up with her playing the piano, pints of beer swilling around on top and everyone singing along. We lived upstairs in a large Victorian house with my aunt and her two grown-up boys living downstairs. It was never quiet and my cousins never needed a reason for a party. My Mum was a strong, independent woman who loved nothing more than having a good time. She taught me well.

I should have really known from the beginning that our marriage was doomed, but we tried to make it work for 15-years. It all came to head one evening with a massive row and he ended up walking out and going back home to his Mum. I think he expected me to run after him, full of apologies and promises that I would change. He expected me to beg him to come home. I didn't!

I knew that if I ever wanted to live my own life in a way that I wanted to, then that was the time to make the break. I didn't want much from life, I just wanted to grow as a person, have fun, learn new things and enjoy life in the best way I could. I would not be able to do that if Denis and I stayed together.

And so we separated. It wasn't particularly amicable, he obviously blamed me and yes, I suppose it was my fault. I wanted to get out of the marriage but he didn't, someone was bound to be hurt.

Jordan was around 5 years old at the time and I felt guilty because his Mum and Dad no longer lived together. Everyone told me that it would be better for him to live with one parent rather than in a house full of hostility and fighting. I'm not sure. Guilt stayed with me for years and, if I'm honest, I still feel it today. I felt guilty because I had hurt my husband. He wasn't a bad man, just not the man for me. I felt guilty because I broke up Jordan's home.

After a few months, it became clear that I couldn't cope financially. Denis had managed to lose his job and wasn't giving me any money at all. I couldn't pay the mortgage plus all the other bills and feed us on what I earned. I was at my wits end and didn't know what to do. It seemed my only option was to go home to Dad and my stepmother which was the last thing I wanted.

It eventually got to the point where I thought I'd reached rock bottom. Jordan was out playing with friends one day and I was sitting on the bottom of the stairs crying my eyes out. Pat came round and announced that she'd come up with a possible solution.

"It's only temporary," she said, "but why don't you and Jordan move in with us until you get back on your feet again?"

She went on to say that they had the space and they would love having Jordan around. I wasn't sure, I didn't want to give up my home. What if living with Pat and Geoff didn't work, I would have nowhere to go. Again, she came up with a solution.

"Rent the house out, that would pay for the mortgage and cover the bills but you would always have somewhere to go back to if it didn't work out."

So that's what we ended up doing.

Now I'm a great believer that the Universe conspires to get you in the right place, at the right time, with the right people. I needed to change my job in order to meet Pat and Geoff, and I needed my marriage to break up in order for Jordan and I to move in with Pat and Geoff, and I needed to be in that position for the rest of my life to change! But hindsight is a wonderful thing, at the time I thought my life was doomed.

Knowing what you don't want is all you need to start the adventure of a lifetime.

A J Leon

June

During that time and all my life changes, Junie was experiencing some of her own. We had already given up as President and Secretary of the church because it was time to hand it over to someone else. We had achieved a lot during our time there but believe that committees need to change every few years to bring in new life and fresh ideas.

We still went to the church whenever we could but as I was living with Pat and Geoff I didn't think it was fair to swan off out and leave them babysitting Jordan. I wasn't unhappy about not being at the church so much, but it was just the way life was changing.

June's life was changing too. I asked her one day if she wanted to go to Church on Sunday as Pat had agreed to babysit. She said she couldn't, she was busy.

"Oh," I said, "what are you up to then?" Our friendship was close enough that I could ask. She faffed about a bit and I knew that whatever she was up to may not be something I liked.

"Right," I replied, "what are you up to?"

"Oh, I'm just going out on Sunday," she told me.

"Who with?" I asked. She didn't answer. I knew then that she was seeing someone else and I couldn't understand why she would tell me. I went through a whole list of men that we both knew and who were possibilities. She kept saying no to them all. I was getting exasperated.

"Who the bloody hell is it? Just tell me," I said.

"David", she replied and wouldn't look at me.

"WHAT????????".

I was totally gobsmacked; how could I not have known? Why the bloody hell had she kept it from me? This was major.

David was a guy we had both worked with at the accountants. He was a nice bloke but the last person on earth that I thought June would go for. He was married and had a son and June was married with a daughter, it had all the makings of becoming very messy.

"Close your mouth," she said, "it's not attractive."

"Fuck attractive," I replied, "you'd better start talking lady, and don't miss anything out".

So, she talked, and talked, and talked. It turned out that she and David found themselves working more and more together. That led to spending lunchtimes together, often going out of the office and that eventually led to evenings spent together. She also told me that she told Dennis, her husband, that she was going out with me on evenings she was seeing David. That was a very dangerous game because he could have asked me at any time and I wouldn't have been able to cover for her. In fact, he did come round to my house one morning and asked if I was with June the night before. Of course, I covered for her, she was my best friend.

During this period of our lives we saw less and less of each other. Eventually she told her husband and David told his wife and they moved in together. June's daughter stayed with her Dad and David's son stayed with his wife, but they both saw their children regularly. Eventually divorces came through, David and June married and were exceedingly happy.

She was busy with her new life and I was busy with mine, plus the fact that once I had moved out of the area, we saw less and less of one another. I missed her. We talked on the phone and I would sometimes go and stay with her for the weekend. She would always get us Pie & Mash.

June's health deteriorated. Looking back, I suppose the signs had always been there but you never really think about losing your best friend, especially at such a young age and when life was really good.

I remember the morning David phoned and told me she had gone. I sat on the stairs and cried and cried. We didn't see each other as often as we used to but I would miss having her in my life.

The Move

I'd settled into my new job well, made a lot of new friends and was enjoying a great social life. I thought that's how my life would be from now on and I was totally happy with that. I missed the church, but I still popped back for the odd service and Pat even came with me from time to time.

But just when you think that everything's running smoothly, the Universe decides it would be a good time to throw the next curve ball into the mix.

The Institute where Pat and I both worked was to close and relocate to Berkshire. I was to be made redundant and Pat would either have to transfer to Berkshire or lose her job!

Fuck!

It wouldn't be immediate, we had a few years to consider our options but nevertheless, decisions would have to be made.

We carried on as normal for a while but our working environment was changing as staff were leaving and going to new jobs. I felt that my perfect life was coming to an end, it was not a nice time.

Pat was a senior scientist and was therefore offered a generous relocation package. I was a secretary and would be made redundant but, because I hadn't been at the Institute that long, the redundancy payment wouldn't be that big. With Pat and Geoff moving away I would have to go back to my house and find another job. But I know I would miss them both terribly and Jordan would be devastated as he had grown to love them very much, they were his family.

"Why don't you move to Berkshire with us?" Pat said one evening, completely out of the blue, as we were relaxing and sipping on glasses of red wine. Bloody hell, where had that come from? It hadn't even entered my mind as an option. What the hell do I do now?

Over the relatively short time that I had known Pat and Geoff, they had become my new family. Pat became the sister I never had and another best friend – how many best friends can one person have, I wonder? As a family, we took Jordan out and about to various places and he was having a lovely childhood. Pat I would go shopping, socialise with friends and do the more 'girlie' things together. I really didn't want that to end at all.

I would have to move away from my Dad and stepmum and, of course, I would be taking Jordan away from his dad. I would be leaving my friends too. But on the other hand, I would only be a couple of hours drive away and could come back often.

I would have to look for a new job if I stayed so I could equally look for a job in a new area. I could sell my house and put the money towards the new one. It was all coming together nicely on the practical front, but what did I really want to do? My heart was singing with the thought of a new start elsewhere and the possibilities it could bring. Eventually I made up my mind: I was going!

Over the next year or so I sold my house and we found a bigger one for all of us in South Oxfordshire. Geoff took voluntary redundancy from his job and found another one within a few months. I was very lucky to get a transfer to the new Institute in Berkshire on a temporary basis but after three months of being there they made my role permanent. Pat moved with some of her colleagues and by April 1992 we were all living in the new house and settling into our new life.

You don't have to see the whole staircase,
just take the first step.

Unknown

Those Opportunities

So, there was another of those opportunities that floated by and I grabbed it. I didn't know whether upping sticks and moving to a place where I knew no one was the right thing to do. How do any of us know whether we're doing the right thing? I was starting to realise that if I went along with my gut instinct it didn't really let me down. OK, it might not always be easy but listening to my own intuition usually meant it would turn out alright in the end.

Many opportunities have floated by me and it's a real art to know which ones to grab and which ones to let go. Many times I tried to do something that I knew deep down wasn't right for me but seemed like a good idea at the time. They never worked. I tried selling books once! I thought it would bring in some extra money for me and Jordan. It was one of those party plan schemes that relied upon people, mainly women, buying a stock of books and then going out and selling them. I bought the books and even got a few bookings for parties. The problem was I am just not a seller, I couldn't sell to save my life. So, the party plan idea fell flat on its face before it even got started and I ended up with a stock of books I didn't want and badly out of pocket.

I learnt a valuable lesson there. I knew I wasn't a natural seller when I started but instead of listening to my intuition I dived in head first. That's another of my problems, I dive in head first without thinking the whole thing through. I remember buying a pool table once on a whim. The guys in the shop managed to get it into my car with the back seats down and tying down the boot, but when I got it home there wasn't anywhere to put it. We managed to get it up in the hall - we have a big square hallway - but there wasn't any extra space to pull the cue back to play the game. It was relegated to the garage and only came out on warm sunny days so Jordan and his friends could play in the garden.

But with age comes a certain amount of wisdom and I learnt to curb my knee-jerk reactions and to take time out to listen to my own intuition. Sometimes my intuition, that gut feeling, is strong and compelling. It pulls me one way or another. Other times it's a bit wishy washy and I'm left unsure.

I was sure about the move to Oxfordshire, I just knew on some deeper level that this would be good for me and Jordan. I weighed up the pros and cons. It was not without its risks, and I would miss my family and friends, but I could see many more opportunities awaiting me if I made the move.

When things aren't working,
the universe is trying to save your ass.

Tracy Kaufmann

Meeting Gill

Life was good once again and I was settled. My job was going well and not too long after the move I was promoted to the Director's PA. We started to become more involved with the social side of work and Pat and I managed to get ourselves on the committee of the Social Club. We picked up from where we left off at the old location and organised some wonderful events for the staff.

During those years of moving and finding a new job my spiritual side was well and truly put on hold. I missed going to the church but then I don't think you need to go to church every week to keep your faith, whatever religion you follow. Although I would say that my spirituality was not a religion, more a way of life. I've been asked many times over the years whether I believe in God. The simple answer is I believe that something far greater than we can ever imagine exists, some call it energy, some call it Source and some call it God. Star Wars referred to it as The Force. Personally, I don't see it as the judge-y God that we must bow down and repent as some organised religions lead us to believe. I would never knock religious faiths, it's a lifeline to many, but I don't follow any particular religion. I was born a Christian, I quite like the idea of Buddhism but I much prefer to follow my own spiritual path, and make my own mind up about it all. Nothing infuriates me more than religious people ramming their faith down my throat. There is a wonderful quote attributed to Dame Maggie Smith that always makes me laugh:

"My dear, religion is like a penis. It's a perfectly fine thing to have and take pride in, but when one takes it out and waves it in front of my face we have a problem."

But at this point in my life the Universe had conspired to get me to the place where I needed to be and with the people I needed to be with, and they weren't finished with me yet! Of course, at the time I didn't give it all much thought, I was too busy just getting on with life. It's only with hindsight that you can see how everything clicks into place. Life was good and, once again, I had no reason to think it would all change. But change it did!

I was working with a lovely young girl, Sonia, and we really gelled from day one. She had a great sense of humour which matched mine and we shared an interest in a lot of similar things.

Over the past few years my ears had blocked several times with excess wax. Yes, yuck I know but bear with me here. Often one, or both, ears would be so solidly blocked that I couldn't hear a thing, just a load of muffled noise. I really was in a world of my own. I'd end up at the doctor's time after time to get them syringed. One morning I said to Sonia that my ears were blocked and I needed to make a doctor's appointment.

"Oh, don't do that," she said, "get them candled, it's much gentler."

What the bloody hell was candling? I'd never heard of it. She went on to tell me that it's an old Indian treatment where they stick lighted candles in your ears and it clears the wax. She said it was safer than syringing which could damage the ear drums. Blimey, who knew these things even existed.

Ok I thought, but how do I find someone to do that for me? I googled, as you do, and there was a woman in the next village who did it. I didn't know her but then I wouldn't know anyone I booked with. With nothing to lose I made an appointment.

I turned up at her house at the appointed time and that was the first time I met Gill. You'll find out much more about her later, but from that first meeting I felt I had known her forever. You know that feeling where you just know that you had met before? There was a familiarity but, in reality, we had never met.

She candled my ears and it was such a lovely relaxing experience, and she cleared the wax. By the time I left we'd spent a lovely hour together, chatting about this and that and all things holistic and spiritual too. There was a common link and the connection I felt was quite strong. I had no idea whether she felt the same, she's never said, but I just knew I would see her again.

Gill told me much later that she had no idea how I found her as she never advertised her treatments at all!

Breast Cancer

My ears continued to block over the next few years and every time I would go back to Gill for a lovely relaxing candling treatment. Gill was a Holistic Therapist and had her own treatment room attached to her home. It was a lovely relaxing space and I loved spending time there. Every time I had a treatment we would spend the hour talking about all things spiritual. We were definitely destined to meet in this lifetime.

Late 2005 I had my first ever routine mammogram. These are done every three years in the UK for women between the ages of 50 and 70. I was just 52 and not expecting anything to show up, so you can imagine my horror when I was called back to the hospital for more tests as the mammogram was unclear. In January 2006 I was diagnosed with breast cancer and there began a gruelling year of surgery, chemotherapy and radiotherapy. If you want to follow my journey with breast cancer then do read my first book *Once Bitten, Twice Prepared.* The book tells not only my breast cancer story but also how my spirituality and personal development over the years was to help greatly.

I continued to go to Gill throughout my cancer treatment and I found reflexology particularly helpful during the gruelling chemotherapy sessions. We continued to chat, and I found that she was the one person that I could be totally myself with and open up about my thoughts, feelings and emotions. Often during times of deeply emotional events and traumas in our lives we find it difficult to express how we truly feel, especially to our nearest and dearest as they too find the whole experience hard and are coping in their own way. Gill was there for me when I needed a shoulder to cry on.

But I got through the year and by the end of 2006 I was ready to get my life back together again and start to have some fun. I had been back at work for a few months and back into the swing of our social programme. We joined a local social club and every Saturday we'd dance the night away. We went on some wonderful holidays and I fell in love with the far east. Life was good once again.

I was hopeful that life would settle down and there would be no more major surprises along the way, and that was certainly the case for a good few years.

I still went to Gill for my ears when I needed to. I loved those sessions, not only were they wonderfully relaxing and cleared my ears of gunk, but Gill and I had some great conversations around all things spiritual. This was as close as I'd come to getting back to spirit since we moved to Oxfordshire and I really didn't want to give that up.

Many years later Gill told me that she had moved to Oxfordshire in the very same year I did. The Universe had a plan for us.

Redundancy

A few years later, probably around 2008, my boss told me one morning that he felt he ought to relocate and be permanently based at our sister institute in Surrey, and he wanted me to go with him.

This was not something I wanted to do. I didn't want to move away from my home and neither did I want to do a 2-hour commute morning and night, five days a week.

"Bugger," he said, "I'm not sure what to do with you then".

"I know what you can do with me," I replied, "make me redundant".

And he did. It took a while as there was a lot of red tape to work through, but eventually I was made redundant. I was about 55 years of age and I felt too young to do nothing at all, but I just wanted something nice and easy without the stress that sometimes came with working at the Institute.

I found a job fairly quickly as the Activities Co-ordinator at a local care home. At that time, the home was mainly for genteel ladies and run by the sisters of St Mary's Convent. It was a lovely gentle place to be and had a spiritual air about the place. I loved being there and enjoyed the job very much. The ladies were lovely, well ok there were the odd one or two which weren't so great, but on the whole I had a lovely time doing all sorts of things and arranging lovely outings with them.

Attached to the home was a chapel where the sisters would go for prayer and I often sat outside and listened to their singing. Now, as you know, I'm not religious at all and if there's one thing that I find very off-putting is others preaching to me about how I should live my life and how I need to let God and Jesus in. But you see, I do strongly believe that there is a stronger force at play and I can feel the energies from Angels, Guides and Spirit. Listening to the sisters singing in the chapel was beautiful and brought with it a sense of peace and serenity.

With the sisters in residence everyone's spiritual needs were catered for. We had a nursing wing attached and inevitably we lost residents as they passed back to the spirit world. But far from the depressing place you might imagine it to be, I saw so much love and some wonderful acts of kindness from the staff and the sisters. As someone's time drew near they were never left alone, the sisters took turns to sit by their bedside. I remember one evening I was working quite late at an event in the Chapel. It was a Welsh Male Voice Choir and our ladies loved it. It was nearing the end and the Choir sang their final song, "Time to Say Goodbye". I felt the swishing of skirts behind me and one of the sisters whispered in my ear "Daphne is about to leave us". Daphne was one of my favourites and yes, I know you shouldn't have favourites but I had a few, and the sister knew I wanted to say my own goodbye. It struck me how appropriate the song was and every time I hear it now I am reminded of the lovely gentle Daphne.

After a year or two the Sisters sold the care home to a company who ran several homes around the country. Inevitably things changed and the staff and residents were not happy, so much so that many of them left. Eventually the sisters went too. Without the sisters, it was not the serene and happy place it once was and I was not enjoying my time there.

I didn't know what I wanted to do, but I knew I was no longer happy. It was time to make a decision!

Do I stay or do I go?

Happiness

During my time at the care home I began to understand that love and happiness were the most important things in life.

Many of us strive to fill our lives with material things thinking they will make us happy – it doesn't. Oh, accumulating stuff may give us a quick high but we quickly lose that feeling and need something else. We're hooked on stuff and always looking for the next fix. I was the same, looking for things to make me happy, the quick fix – just look at the pool table! It made me happy when I bought it but that quickly wore off when I couldn't use it because we didn't have the space. I'm sure I went out and bought something else to replace it.

I loved buying clothes, what woman doesn't? But I would spend stupid amounts of money on clothes that would hang unworn in the wardrobe because either I didn't really like them enough, or didn't really feel comfortable in them, or they were the wrong colour, or they didn't match anything else, or I had gained weight and they didn't fit any more.

And that had gone on for most of my life. I was continually looking for something outside of myself to make me happy. It took working in the care home for me to realise that I'd got it all wrong.

In a place where material possessions were few, there was an abundance of love and friendship between the residents, staff and sisters. They were not looking for material things to bring them pleasure. The simple act of sitting and listening, or holding someone's hand, was often enough to make faces light up. It gave me such joy to see the reaction on some of our residents faces when all I did was sit and listen to their stories. That joy far surpassed any good feelings I got from buying new stuff.

There is so much happiness to be gained from the simple things, the natural things, in life. The more love and kindness you give, the more will come flowing back to you.

Life is quite simple really, but we make it so complicated and difficult. I would often sit and listen to my Dad's stories of the war years and how they would sit down the air raid shelter for hours on end and just sit and talk. They didn't have much, and what they did have had a high chance of being destroyed during the bombing. But they had each other, they had the camaraderie and the whole ethos of looking out for each other. My Dad's home was bombed so they salvaged what they could and moved in with his sister's husband's family. Can you imagine how cramped that house must have been? Dad later told me that some of his happiest times was during those awful war years.

Reiki

Many years ago, at the Spiritualist Church I was active with the healing work and at one point I was told by a very good healer that I would be taking a break from healing soon but I would eventually return to it. I'm not sure I believed him at the time but little did I know then that my life was about to completely change again.

Here I was ensconced in my new life and in a new place. I had taken a week off work but we decided to just stay at home and relax. One afternoon I was doing some ironing and watching Escape to the Country on TV. The couple wanted a large house in the country with an annex so the woman could start her Reiki Practice.

"You could do that," said Pat, who was watching the programme with me. She had planted the seed.

I mulled it over. Reiki is a method of healing, using the natural life force energy that surrounds and runs through all of us. It is deeply relaxing and helps to shift any unwanted and negative energies, allowing the body to return to its natural balance.

Learning to do Reiki really struck a chord and I could feel my excitement start to grow at the thought of it. Whether I could turn it into a business was another matter though, but a possibility and one that could help me to leave a job that I was growing more and more unhappy with. However, I didn't have a clue how to go about it and then thought about Gill and wondered if she could possibly teach me.

My ears were starting to block so a great excuse to book an appointment with her. This time was different though and proved to be my turning point. As I lay on the couch and she placed a candle in my ear, I heard the words in my head "how many times do we have to block your ears to get you to listen?"

Bloody hell, where did that come from?

I talked to Gill about Reiki, although she couldn't teach me she gave me the name of someone who could. It was up to me to take the next step.

Quite often Reiki Masters will say "you don't choose to do Reiki, Reiki chooses you". When I left Gill that day I knew that Reiki had chosen me and that I was about to start a new adventure, and one that would involve Gill. Don't ask me how I knew, I just knew.

The Universe works in magical ways to get you to the right place, at the right time to connect you with the right people.

When the student is ready, the teacher will appear

Buddha

Reiki Training

When I got home I immediately Googled the name of the Reiki Master that Gill had given to me and was absolutely gobsmacked to see that she was running a Level 1 training course the following week. I wondered if she would still have space at this late stage but reasoned that if I was meant to train in Reiki then she would have a space.

Although I had taken several years out of my spiritual journey, I still did a lot of reading and questioning and with the internet and social media much more widely available it was much easier to learn.

I mentioned earlier that healing is really about intent and focus, but you still need some level of training to know how to go about it. Reiki training is carried out over three, or sometimes four levels. Reiki level one is all about the self and we learn to look after our own health and wellbeing. Level two is about giving healing to others and level 3 is about becoming a Reiki Master and teaching others, although sometimes this is taught over two separate levels.

I phoned my new potential Reiki Master and asked whether she had space on her next level 1 course the following week and yes, she did, so I booked immediately. I was delighted and excited that not only had I got a place on the course but also that I was getting back to some sort of spiritual development.

My new Reiki Master lived a 20-minute or so drive away and I turned up at her house on the morning of my training all bright eyed and bushy tailed. There was just one other person on the course that day and Catherine, the Reiki Master, told us that she liked to keep it small to be able to give more individual attention and for each of us to gain the maximum we could from the day. What an amazing day it was, we were attuned to Reiki, taught the principles of healing, meditated and finally showed how to give a self-treatment. We then had to start a 21-day period of self-healing and report back.

I spent the following 21-days on such a rollercoaster of experiences. Some days were brilliant and I learnt a lot, other days I didn't think I was getting it at all and wondered if I could be any good at healing.

I completed the 21-days and went back to Catherine for the second part of Level I training.

"All perfect," she eventually said, as she handed me my certificate.

"Now I want you to continue working on yourself and incorporate Reiki into your daily regime and way of life."

Bloody hell, what did she mean by that? I didn't have a daily regime, I just bumbled my way through life. Should I start a daily regime, and if I should then what should it be? I thought about it for a while but all I could come up with was self-Reiki and meditation. Was that enough? Well, it was a start and I could build on that if and when I needed to.

"When can I do level 2?" I asked Catherine.

"Not for a minimum of 3-months," she said, "but 6-months would be better."

Oh shit, I didn't want to wait that long, but I didn't have a choice.

I kept in touch with the girl that I trained with. She wanted to go on to level 2 as well so we agreed that when the 3-months was up we would badger Catherine again to book us in for more training.

In the meantime, I carried on with my self-Reiki and a little meditation. I must admit that my meditation was a little hit and miss. I found it hard, especially doing it alone. I was ok in a guided meditation but when my mind was left to its own devices it would simply wander off and not want to come back.

One of the big problems I've always had is patience, or my lack of it. I want everything yesterday. If I want to do something I don't want to wait until I have worked through the process. I want to start and master it in the shortest possible time.

I was the same with Reiki – I wanted to get to Master Teacher in a couple of weeks! Was never going to happen. My Reiki Master did her best to reign me in, my guides were even better – they just would not let me progress until I was ready. I knew there were, and still are, lots of internet sites out there that promise Reiki Master/Teacher attunements in just one weekend but that just didn't sit right with me.

I knew what my goal was – I wanted to be able to give and teach Reiki to as many people as possible and I wanted to be able to do it the following week. I begged, pleaded, ranted and raved but to no avail. It wasn't that my motives were bad, they weren't, I was just not ready yet.

That was hard for me because of my natural urge to steam ahead and just get on with it. It was a big lesson and I had a hard time learning it. I try to listen more now.

Reiki, like a lot of things in life, is not something to rush at. Learning, like Reiki, does not have an end, we do it constantly whether we are aware of it or not. Life is one big classroom – every day something new comes into our lives. It comes in many forms, something we read, something we watch on TV, something someone tells us. We need to slow down, look, listen and learn. If we go full steam ahead, we miss the journey. We will never learn if we are blinkered and can only see the goal. Yes, we can aspire to our goals and we will reach them, but in the fullness of time, when we are fully ready.

I knew that if I became a Reiki Master Teacher the following day I would be the very best Master Teacher that I knew how to be. However, if I waited a while, learned a lot more, I would be even better! If I were to teach others, then they deserved the best they could get.

But don't give up on your dreams just because you can't do it immediately – think how much better it will be when you do eventually realise them. You will have more experience, more knowledge, more confidence and will be in a far better position to meet the challenges that your goal will bring. Above all, enjoy the journey – it has much to teach you.

Mmmmm, that all seems a bit deep, doesn't it, but well worth mulling over.

Having said all that, when the three months passed I did ask Catherine if she would do our level two training and she agreed. She booked us in for the following month which, in my opinion, was far too long to wait. Patience is not my strong point, when I decide to do something I just want to get on with it. I'm sure this is one of my life lessons because I have been made to wait for many things during my life.

Eventually Level two training was completed and I could treat others. Woohoo, I couldn't wait to get out there and heal the world! I still had to complete another 21-days of self-Reiki but in addition I could use my family and friends to practice on. Eventually I gained my certificate.

I asked when I could do Level Three.

"The longer you practice at this level the better," said Catherine, "but definitely no sooner than 3-months."

It was during my Reiki II attunement I had the feeling of someone standing at my right shoulder. Ooooer, this was new, I hadn't experienced this feeling before and wondered if it might be a new guide, here to help me specifically with Reiki. I mentioned it to Catherine and she confirmed that there was indeed someone standing just behind my right shoulder. She suggested that, during a self-Reiki session, I ask for a name and who they are.

During my session the next day I asked the guide to come and help me and asked if I could be told the name and a little more about them. Again, I felt a very strong presence of someone just behind my right shoulder and this time had a feeling around my chin and neck, as if I was wearing something. That was it, no name and still none the wiser as to who my new guide was.

The following morning, in that lovely moment where you're not quite asleep but you're not really awake either, I saw words that looked like "St Wendra of Dreda". I was a bit taken aback, where did that come from and what did it all mean? I googled and was absolutely gobsmacked on the hits I got – amongst them was the following:

St. Wendreda was the daughter of seventh-century King Anna, one of the earliest Christian kings. At a time when Christianity was putting down roots among the Anglo-Saxon peoples of England, St. Wendreda and her sisters, Etheldred and Sexburga, were enthusiastic missionaries spreading the Gospel of Christ.

Shunning the life of a princess, Wendreda dedicated herself to healing. She eventually settled in a small settlement called Mercheford, where some humble fisherman resided. Her sister, Etheldred, went on to found the monastery at Elyl, while her other sibling, Sexburga, became abbess of a monastery in Minster.

Later, Wendreda founded a community at March, Cambridgeshire, dedicated to healing. She passed peacefully into the heavenly kingdom, and her relics, enshrined in gold, were buried in the Ely Cathedral.

However, in 1016, the relics were carried off in battle in the hopes they would bring victory. At the Battle of Ashingdon, the conquering Danish king, a pagan, seized the relics, but soon was converted to Christianity. He took the relics to the Canterbury Cathedral where they rested for the next 300 years.

In 1343, St. Wendreda was returned to March and enshrined in the church dedicated to her memory. The St. Wendreda Church stands to this day, and is world famous for its magnificent double-hammer beam roof along with 120 carved angels.

Not only was that so mind-blowing for me but, as a keen genealogist, I had traced my paternal family back to March in Cambridgeshire! A few years later I went to March and visited her church.

It took me a year to complete all my Reiki training and I was so proud when I received my Reiki Master certificate. Not only could I get out there and heal the world but I could teach the world how to heal itself too.

Oh, my naiveté knew no bounds. It took me a long time to learn that some people didn't want to be healed and they certainly didn't want to heal themselves.

Thoughts Around Healing

I don't really get on too well with our feathered friends. I don't know why – my friends will tell you that I must have had a traumatic experience in the past which involved a bird. Arrrrgggghhhh! They think I should go for therapy - no way !!!!!!!!!!

I remember when I was pregnant with Jordan I was lying on a lounger in the garden one day and a little bird landed on the washing line above me. He lost his balance and fell into my lap and I went into panic as it flapped about trying to right itself. I knocked the bird one way as I fell off the lounger the other way. I know I was screaming because my neighbours came out to see what was wrong. But it would happen to me, wouldn't it?

I would never harm a bird – I just don't want them near me. But they seem to seek me out, I think I must have a target on my head or something. The bigger birds are not too bad, they're not as flappy and hyperactive as the smaller ones. I can just about tolerate ducks, and emus and ostriches have quite a manic charm about them.

So it was no surprise that, on holiday some time ago, a bird with a gammy leg sought me out. This was not just a 10-minute thing, oh no, no, no, it went on for three days! Every day, as I settled down on my sunbed, along it limped and settled right next to me. I tried to encourage it to move to someone far better than I to give it comfort, but it didn't want anyone else, just me. I was unnerved to say the least, I couldn't settle and had visions of it leaping up onto my lap.

It was a poor little thing though and I did feel very sorry that it was injured. It didn't seem to be able to fly, just hopped around a bit on one leg and then rested. Pat and I debated about what to do. We were in the Far East so knew that a vet was probably out of the question. Pat fed it and gave it water and I did the only thing I could – I gave it Reiki.

Now, I wonder whether this little bird knew on some level that I could help a bit. It sat perfectly still while I gave him his daily dose of Reiki and, although he wasn't cured, he was looking a lot perkier by the third day. His hopping around became a bit quicker and he even flew a couple of feet.

I wish I could give you a happy ending here, but we had to leave for home and I have no idea what happened to him. I did the best I could and just have to trust that the little bird is where he should be.

During the last few minutes on my sunbed before we had to leave, a bird (not him) flew over and left a deposit on my head – I'm still debating whether this was a thank you for helping his friend or was he telling me it was time to leave?

Counselling

During the 21-days after my Reiki Level II training I could treat family and friends as long as I didn't charge for my services. It will come as no surprise that I had many willing bodies to practice on during that period.

One morning I was treating a friend at home when another idea floated by me. This friend had a lot of issues which had been buried deep for many years. Those issues needed to be dealt with and released if he was to ever find peace but at that time he admitted that he was scared to start peeling away those layers because of what he might have to deal with.

It occurred to me at that time that although I could give Reiki that would certainly help to peel away the layers and heal what lay beneath, I had no idea on how to deal with someone who was opening up on all sorts of issues. In my ignorance I could possibly do more harm than good.

I decided to take a counselling course and enrolled at my local college. It was Level 1, 1-year evening classes and I was quite excited about the prospect of not only learning something new but something that would be beneficial to my clients.

It was heavy! We had to do the theory before we could get to the practical. I wanted to skip that bit and just get on with it. Typical of me, I wanted to dive in head first and get on with the nitty gritty stuff. I was the same when we used to do our shows and pantomimes at work – forget rehearsals, let's just do it!

Nearly every week for a year I would set off for college, spend 2-hours in the classroom and then come home with loads of research and homework to be done. Not everyone who enrolled on the course stuck with it, and I will admit that I nearly gave up several times, but Pat spurred me onwards and gave me the confidence that I could do it. I made friends along the way and we encouraged one another when the going got tough. It was also nice to be with people who had a common aim – to pass the exam!

I loved the work and I particularly loved it when we got to the practical stuff. However, I found it difficult at first to keep quiet and listen! There is an art to drawing stuff out of people and phrasing open-ended questions without adding in any form of suggestion. We practiced time and time again on a 1-2-1 basis and we role played as a group. Our practical sessions were videoed for part of our final assignment.

The course was assignment based and I had a deadline that I needed to submit by. I would sit for hours and days bashing away at my computer, trying to get this assignment written. Eventually I submitted and just had to sit and wait for the results.

At last the envelope popped through my door - I had passed! I also had an e-mail from my tutor congratulating me and asking if I would like to go on and do the next level as he felt I had a natural aptitude for it. I thought about it for a while but eventually decided not to continue. For one thing, I never wanted to be a counsellor *per se* but to simply use the skills with my Reiki clients, and secondly there were so many other subjects I wanted to study.

Learning

Learning never stops. I'd heard that expression many times and I used to think it was a load of rubbish. When I was younger, learning to me was school days and the subjects we were made to learn. I hated school. Some subjects I liked but there were more that I hated. I really could not see the point of sitting for what seemed like hours on end trying to get to grips with trigonometry when I was hardly likely to need it when I left school.

As I got older I came to realise that learning is indeed a lifelong thing. Whether it's taking some organised courses or simply from the school of life.

A few years after leaving school I went off to college and took courses in typing and secretarial work. I later went on to study for a Diploma in Administration and Administrative Procedures. I really enjoyed those courses and achieved high grades. I realised that I managed all that because I loved what I was being taught. It also had a means to an end, not only with the knowledge I gained but the qualifications were instrumental in my gaining promotion. Added to that was the fact that the tutors treated us all as the adults we were and I realised for the first time that they were normal people too and just imparting the knowledge that they already had.

When I did my Reiki training I became passionate about the journey this would take me on. Not only was I learning about how to give healing, but it had the huge potential of helping others. I was also learning a lot about myself. Reiki had reignited my spiritual journey and I was beginning to realise that I still had so much to learn.

I went on to take many courses over the years, some I loved whilst others not so much, and all those courses gave me the basic knowledge that I needed to get going in the direction I wanted to head. But the real learning started when I put that basic knowledge into practise.

Yes, you can be given the basic guidelines and parameters to apply but every person, situation and experience is different and totally unique. So, you are constantly adding your unique experiences of each situation to the basic teachings and writing your own manual, as it were. It never stops.

The other thing I've come to understand is that all knowledge, courses, etc, is never wasted. There are times when what I have learnt in the past and put aside comes back into use when I take a new direction in life.

Who knows, trigonometry might raise its head again one day!

Reiki Share Group

I wanted to run my own therapy business but didn't have a clue where to start. I had nowhere to practice from and no idea how to attract clients.

I started by trying to find a place where I could work from. I went to several businesses around our town to see if they had a room I could rent. A couple did, but they wanted me to sign up for 6-months to a year's rental and quite honestly, I just couldn't afford to do that. I needed to know that I had some money coming in to offset the rent.

I decided to go mobile so I bought a therapy couch, covers, pillows and everything else I thought I might need. I told family and friends and I managed to pick up a few bookings. However, being mobile didn't really work out that well for me. Lugging the heavy therapy couch in and out of the car, and sometimes upstairs, was starting to play havoc with my shoulders. I had to contend with working in someone else's space which was often busy and cluttered and not the tranquil place I wanted my client to receive their therapy session in. I had to contend with pets running in and out and around my feet. One evening a cat flew into the room, jumped up onto the couch and onto my client's stomach, she yelled as claws dug into her flesh and the cat squealed and hissed at me! Don't get me wrong, I am a big animal lover and have cats of my own, but that little poppet completely ruined the peace and tranquillity. I think the crunch came when at one home the kids were in and out asking for biscuits, drinks, asking their mum what she was doing before finally plonking themselves down on the sofa and putting on the TV.

I was so upset, surely that couldn't be the end of my becoming a Reiki Therapist before I had even really started.

I remembered that at one point during my training Catherine suggested that I might like to consider starting a Reiki Share Group. These were particularly good for practice and pulling Reiki people together. This seemed like sound advice. If I was going to teach I would want something in place to offer my students. That was great, but I still had to find people to come!

We were soon going on holiday so I decided I would take that time to consider how I was going to make it happen. I asked my guides for help and set the intent that I needed someone to join my Reiki Share Group and left it at that.

Our holiday took us off to the Far East and we visited many wonderful places. I love South East Asia, I love the people and the culture. We visited many Buddhist temples during that trip but the one that sticks in my memory was Kek Lok Si in Penang. Kek Lok Si is the largest Buddhist temple in Malaysia and stands on a hilltop at Air Itam, near Penang Hill. The complex is divided into three zones with the beautiful gardens at the base complete with a turtle liberation pond; the middle section has temples, gardens, a pagoda and the four heavenly kings pavilion; and the hilltop plays host to an enormous statue of the Goddess of Mercy, Kuan Yin. At the time, I had no idea who Kuan Yin was and I certainly had no idea that I would work with her over the coming years in a healing capacity. Isn't it just amazing how spirit and the universe works?

Anyway, I digress a bit. It was during my time in Penang that one morning, I was relaxing on the beach and decided to check my e-mails. There was a message from a lady who lived in my home town asking if I knew of any Reiki Share Groups she could join. Wow, Spirit didn't hang about, did they?

I replied immediately saying that I was away but would sort something out when I got home. This was the push I needed to put my thoughts into action. I spent the rest of the holiday trying to think through the logistics of how I was going to start my Group, could I get another couple of people interested and where I would hold it.

When I got home I called Gill and asked if she would be interested in joining. She agreed immediately AND offered her treatment room as a venue. I went back to the lady who made the original request, gave her the details and she asked if she could bring someone with her. All my problems were solved in one go.

My guides had come up trumps for me once again. The organisation all fell into place nicely and they directed two of the loveliest people my way. Not forgetting, of course, my lovely Gill who is always there for me.

So if you need some help, ask your guides. They always listen and are always ready and willing to help - if, of course, it's in your best interests!

We continued to meet once a month, just the four of us. We worked really well together and the energy was amazing. We all agreed that what we had was special and that there was so much potential within the group. We spent as much time talking about spiritual development as we did sharing Reiki. All four of us were, or nearly, Reiki Masters and as such wanted to explore and develop our spiritual awareness. And so, the concept of a "Spiritual Development Group" was born.

We all agreed that the Reiki Shares should continue, and grow, as we recognised this was a vital part of our development too. We opened the Group to anyone trained in Reiki and it wasn't long before we had more people than could comfortably fit into Gill's therapy room. We eventually moved over to the local village hall which had all the space we needed plus a large car park.

Within a short space of time we had not only a good, and growing, Reiki Share Group but also an exciting Spiritual Development Group.

Just Ask

We say quite often 'you only have to ask' but to some, asking can be a hard thing to do. I have a problem asking for help. Why is that I wonder. Is it my upbringing, society, our culture? I sort of believe that if you want something, or something doing, you just have to get on and do it yourself.

Recently I came home from hospital after surgery and needed a period of rest and recovery whilst I got my strength and mobility back. My family and friends were fabulous and I got the standard 'if you want anything just ask'. Pat was particularly good because she anticipated my every need but even with that there were still a couple of things I had to ask for help with. But I didn't like asking, I didn't like bothering other people and I felt I should be doing it myself.

But it doesn't have to be like that, does it? I learned quite early on my spiritual pathway that if you want help from spirit you do have to ask. After all, how does the universe know what you want if you don't ask. And that goes for people too, how does anyone know what you want help with unless you ask?

You see, from a spiritual perspective we all have free will and if the Universe, our guides, Angels etc just simply barge in with what they know to be right for us, it goes against our free will. Yes, what they want to do for us, or make available to us, is absolutely the right thing but we need to be ready to accept.

When we ask then we're ready and the Universe will do all in its power to make it happen, so long as it's for our highest good.

As soon as I asked for help with the Reiki Share Group, everything fell into place and worked out exactly how it should.

I still ask and trust that everything will work out for me. If it doesn't then I know it is not meant to be.

I still have a problem asking my friends and family for help though, so something I still need to work on.

The Children

It was around this time that Gill invited me along to the clinic she ran for children with special needs. The children were given Bowen treatments once a month which helped them immensely with different aspects of their needs and she wondered whether I would like to join them and give Reiki.

The clinic received no financial support, just relied upon donations and fund-raising events that Gill and her team organised. Everyone gave their time for free.

Off I went on that first Saturday morning not knowing what to expect. Gill and the other therapist were working with two children, two ladies were dealing with the Admin, parents were waiting with their children and one little girl was having a wonderful time constantly running up and down the hall. Gill asked me to try giving some Reiki to the little girl to get her to calm down enough to receive Bowen's therapy. A tall order, considering she had not stopped since I had been in the hall. But I sat down and just let the Reiki flow into the room hoping that she would take a little. After a while she started to slow down and came over to the couch and let her Mum lift her onto it. A couple of seconds later she flung herself into my arms and I was completely lost. She didn't stay, but she had made her point. She got me hook, line and sinker! She eventually calmed down enough to get her Bowen's treatment and some more Reiki.

I spent the rest of the morning giving Reiki to the children as and where I felt pulled. The children were delightful, each different and with different needs but all shining brightly. I made the Reiki available to them and I never felt any of them blocking it. They all got their Bowen's treatments and went on their way. I strongly felt that their parents would have benefited greatly from a little Reiki too, but that was for another time.

The work that Gill and her team did was fantastic. Although the children were receiving their conventional medical care, the holistic therapies really enhanced their wellbeing and the parents received much needed support in a non-medical, relaxed and fun setting.

I had an enjoyable morning and all I had to do was give a few hours of my time and make the Reiki available. It was that simple. I continued with the clinic for several years until it closed around 2016.

Angels? Yeah Right!!

I'd been very spiritual for around 30-odd years, and had a lot of beliefs that many find spooky and, well, a bit potty. That's ok. At times, even Jordan would say that I was doing my woo-woo stuff. As long as we keep an open mind, then acceptance will come when we are ready for it. I like to think of myself as a normal, level-headed and two-feet-on-the-ground kind of person, so I will admit that I do tend to step back from the more "airy-fairy" beliefs. I tended to draw the line at what I would call "fanciful" things – like Angels!

Whilst I was doing my Reiki training my Reiki Master was constantly banging on about angels and I used to think she had lost the plot a bit.

Once I completed my Reiki training I started to read everything I could on healing and energy and I just about exhausted our local library! But one particular afternoon I picked up *Healed by an Angel* by Jacky Newcomb. I have no idea why I took that book - it was not something I would normally go for. It was more than likely that there weren't many spiritual books to choose from that afternoon, but it certainly was a book that I needed to read at that time. I will admit it was a lovely book that told individual stories of healing and spiritual experiences. At the start of the book the author tells how we all have spirit guides and helpers, and angels. Well spirit guides and helpers I fully accepted and yes, I certainly have my fair share of these. But angels – hmmmmm. The author went on to say that you can communicate with your angel, find out their name and sometimes they leave little gifts, especially small white feathers. Really? That's a bit far-fetched surely!

OK – nothing ventured, nothing gained so one day when I was alone in the house I sat down and concentrated and pictured an angel. It was the normal type of angel that you find on top of the Christmas Tree because that's what my idea of an angel is. I felt someone draw in close but that's not unusual for me, so I asked for a name. *Peachy* came straight into my head. Really? Oh, for God's sake, what was I doing? So, I questioned that and immediately got "Yup, just Peachy". I was overwhelmed by the greatest feeling of love, which again is not unusual but was this really an angel? The song playing on the radio at that time was John Lennon's "Woman" and the lyrics "I love you" repeated two or three times.

All very lovely but was this really an angel? My angel? But I wasn't ruling it out and all day long I found myself having quiet little words with "Peachy". I remember at one point I said something along the lines of "Ok Peachy, if you're real then leave me a sign".

I went up to bed that night and, as usual, the first stop was the bathroom. There on the floor was a little white feather!!!!

The lyrics to Abba's "I Have a Dream" came to mind:

I believe in Angels
Something good in everything I see
I believe in Angels
When I know the time is right for me

The time was definitely right for me.

Thoughts Around Angels

I love working with the Angels and over the years I took several different courses on working with Angels and Archangels. One of the highlights was meeting Kyle Grey, author and spiritual teacher who really knows his stuff where angels are concerned.

But long before I knew what I know now, I had this experience.

I met Jane in November and we got chatting about this and that. She told me that she had been having problems with a "presence" in her house and it was affecting her children. Her young son, James, was having real problems sleeping and had started refusing to go to bed at night because of these people in his room. Jane resorted to letting her younger child, Jessica, sleep in the same room to give James a little comfort, but it was far from ideal. Jessica started to refer to the people as James' friends and it became apparent that she could sense them too but didn't seem quite so bothered by them as James. Jane's husband was totally freaked out by the whole thing and wouldn't even discuss it.

When I met Jane, she was at the end of her tether and didn't know what to do to make these "people" leave. She, too, could feel their presence and had asked them to leave but to no effect. I explained that, in my experience, these people lingered close to property and earthly things because they couldn't accept that they were dead and they didn't know how to leave or what to do next. It usually took someone who knew what they were doing to coax the "people" to leave and to guide them onwards. As it happened, Jane knew someone who was a medium and so I suggested she ask her to visit the house and see if she could help in any way.

It was about this time that my introduction to the Archangels began. It seemed everywhere I went, signs from the Angels were leaping out at me. Now I wasn't sure about these Angels but I did a little research on the internet and discovered that there were many of them and they all have their own specific work to do. Archangel Michael protects and cuts the ties of things that we no longer need; Archangel Raphael is the healer and Archangel Gabriel is the teacher and messenger. There are many more angels who all have their own jobs to do, but they can only help us if we ask them to as they cannot impose on our own free will. Hummmm!

I began to think more about these angels and I will admit to asking Archangel Raphael to help with a couple of my own health issues, all with good outcomes. I started to wonder if Archangel Michael might be able to help with Jane's problem and help to lead James' "friends" to where they needed to be. But then I thought that if I mentioned it to her she would think I'd lost the plot and we wouldn't speak again. But this kept nagging at me, I wanted to help this family and the little boy who was being troubled and afraid to go to sleep in case these "people" took him away. After all, I knew how he felt as I'd had a similar experience with Granddad's picture in my bedroom when I was a child.

I next saw Jane and the children just before Christmas. Nothing had changed and she hadn't felt she could ask her Medium friend for help. I also met her husband and he admitted that he was totally freaked out by the whole thing. Although he couldn't feel anything, he wasn't at all happy with the effect it was having on his family.

Archangel Michael popped into my mind and I found myself blurting it out to Jane – this was a bit bizarre as I hadn't decided at that point to say anything. I explained to Jane what Michael could do and told her to ask him to help in cutting the earthly ties of these "people" so that they could go on their way and take the next step in their journey. We agreed she had nothing to lose so yes, she said she would give it a try.

Jane and I met some time later and her first words were "your Archangel Michael worked". It seems their "people" had left the house and the family have no more problems. James is sleeping much better and he also asks Michael for protection.

I am overjoyed that it worked for them as a family and little James is no longer troubled. Of course, I am also very pleased to have proof that Archangel Michael is a) out there somewhere and b) answers our requests. Yes, I know I shouldn't need proof but sometimes we all have a few little wobbles. I must just add here that Archangel Michael is not mine – he is here for everyone, but you do have to ask him for help.

Jane also told me that she is now so keen to explore and discover all things spiritual that she has joined a meditation group and, at her first session, had such an amazing experience.

So, if you need protection, healing and guidance – all you need to do is ask!

The Brain Scan

One morning as I got out of bed I started to feel a tingling sensation in my head and down the left side of my face. I rubbed away at it but it didn't go.

Bloody hell, I'm having a stroke were my immediate thoughts. But the tingling didn't change. I ran to the bathroom mirror and I looked perfectly normal, my mouth hadn't drooped and I could raise both arms. Probably not a stroke then.

After a while it wore off. Phew, I was ok and it was just one of those random weird things that happen from time to time.

No, not random because it happened again that evening. Shit, what do I do? It wore off but happened again the following morning. I was getting really scared now, there was something seriously wrong with me.

I told Pat, mainly because I was scared but also because I knew that she would make me go to the doctor and get it checked out. There's no messing about with Pat, when she decides you need to do something then the easiest way is to just get on and do it.

I made an appointment and off I went. It wasn't my own GP as she was on holiday and, although the doctor I saw was good, I wanted the comfort of my own doctor. He asked me loads of questions and ended the consultation by saying that he didn't know what was wrong but seeing that it was not too long after my breast cancer diagnosis and treatment he would refer me to a Neurologist at the hospital.

Fucking shitting pissing bloody hell, now I had a sodding brain tumour!

"That's not what he's saying", said Pat. "He's just being cautious because of your previous history."

I got the appointment within the week. Bloody hell, that was quick. He must have had serious concerns and marked the referral urgent. By now I was convinced there was something serious going on in my head as the tingling kept coming.

Off I went and saw a lovely lady doctor who asked me reams of questions. She went on to say that she thought it might possibly be migraines just presenting themselves in a different way, but to be on the safe side and because of my previous history she would refer me for a brain scan. As soon as she got the results we would talk again.

Fuck, fuck, fuckety fuck, I do have a brain tumour!

I had the scan within a couple of days. That really wasn't too bad at all, but the wait for the results was horrible.

Two days later I got a phone call from the neurologist. *Shitting hell, they've found something*, were my first thoughts when she told me who it was calling. I could feel my whole body going into the flight or fight mode as that cold grip of fear got me in the stomach and I suddenly needed the loo!

"I thought you would like to know as soon as possible," she started. "I've got your brain scan results back and it all looks normal. So, I really do think that your tingling is just migraines, but if you notice any changes then you need to come back."

Oh boy, was I relieved! I didn't have a brain tumour after all but neither did I think it was a migraine.

The tingling continued but not as often. One particular time, I was just getting ready for bed and they started. *Oh, no not again*, I thought and then I heard in my head "hello"!

"WHAT!!!!"

It turned out that the tingling happened when an angel was present. I hadn't even considered that as a possibility because I was so convinced I had a brain tumour. Many years later I was to tell someone this story only to have her say that a very similar thing happened to her but she thought she was having a string of mini-strokes!

My Reiki Practice

The Reiki Share Groups continued and more and more people were coming along. I didn't realise there were so many Reiki Therapists in our area.

One evening, it felt like we stepped up a notch and moved on to a whole new level. I didn't know if that kind of thing happened in other shares, but we all felt that it was more than just giving and receiving Reiki that evening.

The energy was high and we all felt a lot of activity in the room. Reiki was flowing and I felt the energy like I never have before. What was amazing was how we all felt so connected, that we worked as one rather than individuals. Then three things happened.

We became aware that we had a lot of spirit observers present. They wanted us to know that they were extremely grateful to us for doing what we were doing and that, although we had free will, we had chosen to spend our evening working in this way. They reminded us that gratitude worked both ways. I felt really humbled.

The second thing to happen gave us slight cause for concern as we all felt, to varying degrees, that there was someone present who we felt shouldn't really be there. We wondered how he had got through when we had been so particular about protection. But, it turned out, he was not harmful in any way – just extremely pompous and arrogant. He was a master healer and appeared to be on one massive ego trip so he had been brought to us to observe and learn. As soon as we recognised him for what he was, he left.

The final thing that happened was that I became aware of a bus pulling up and loads of people getting off. They stood milling around watching us and appeared to be waiting for something. We finished working and formed a circle to give thanks and close ourselves down. It was at that point that we directed Reiki to the people from the bus and bathed them in white light. They got back on the bus and went on their way. Most strange.

So a most unusual evening, but what an amazing one. Not only had we each given and received Reiki, we had helped the arrogant man on an ego trip, we had bathed a bus load of people in Reiki energy and while light, and we had received grateful thanks from the higher beings.

But whilst the Reiki Shares were growing and eventful, my own thoughts of running a Reiki Therapy business were dwindling. I was finding it more and more difficult to find a place to work from let alone attracting clients, and I started to wonder whether I was meant to be doing this kind of work at all. Other people seemed to be thriving so maybe it was me.

I had given Reiki to a few people but I was never going to earn the living from it. Things were not going as I planned. This gave rise to some serious self-doubt. Oh, I knew that Reiki worked, I knew that I could channel it, but for some reason no-one wanted me to channel it to them!! What was wrong with me?

It took me a long while to realise that nothing was wrong with me, I was just approaching it in the wrong way. I presumed that I could decide what I wanted to do and all would be well – wrong again.

Some deep thinking followed and slowly I began to realise that I didn't control the way I was to work. Oh yes, I had free will but when I tried to exercise it I was just getting nowhere. I had to move in a different direction, and when I realised that I began to recognise the opportunities that appeared and I acted upon them. I didn't know if it would work or not, but if I didn't try I would never know.

I didn't think it was ever an ego thing, but more one of control. I've always wanted to be in control of my life, to plan and know what the outcome will be! I've always found it difficult to just 'go with the flow'.

Reiki was, and still is, right for me, but I just needed to use it in a different way to how I expected it to be.

I never did run a Reiki Practice, but what I did was so much more than I ever expected. I just had to get out of my own way and let my guides and the universe steer me in the right direction.

My Son

I have just one son, Jordan, and I love him beyond reason. He's a man now, but will always be my baby. Now I'm sure at this point all you Mums out there are in total agreement, so you'll understand how I felt when he announced that he was off to Brazil for six months.

Of course, I didn't want him to go, he was in his early 20s at that time and Brazil was on the other side of the world, all sorts of nasty things could happen. And, to be completely honest, I was afraid that he would meet a nice Brazilian girl and want to stay!

But I never really had a say in the matter and, to be honest, neither should I have. He was an adult, it was his life and he had every right to make his own decisions without any angst being put on him by an overbearing mother. But that didn't stop me crying buckets when we said goodbye, or constantly worrying about him.

Within my spiritual development, I know that attachment is not good and that we all have to deal with separation at some point in our lives. As mothers, we all know the pain of separation, even an hour away from our new-born is difficult. We constantly feel that we shouldn't be too far away in case we are needed. As a spouse and partner the pain is immense when separation takes place after a lifetime together.

I do believe, however, that separation is only temporary – at some point we will be re-united. But knowing and feeling are two different things. We are living in the here and now and the pain of what we must cope with is often very difficult.

But Jordan had to live his life and I had to live mine. I enjoy every moment we spend together and when we're apart I look forward to the next time he's back.

One morning I woke up to an e-mail from him with the subject line "Coming Home". He had booked his return flight and I was so so excited. And then he sent me another e-mail!

At that time, Skype was the only means of face-to-face conversation but even that was hit and miss and depended on good internet connections. E-mail was the way we communicated but it wasn't instant, there was the time difference for one thing and then I had to wait for him to go to an internet café to read his messages.

Anyway, his e-mail said that there might be a bit of a problem as his visa had run out several weeks previously so he had overstayed his time in Brazil. He was worried that they might stop him at the airport!

Oh, for God's sake, why on earth didn't he check it? Once he left for the airport I would have no way of contacting him and he definitely wouldn't message me. I worried all day and had visions of the Brazilian authorities throwing him into jail for outstaying his welcome in their country.

That night I went to bed and sent Reiki to the situation. I asked for a good outcome for all concerned and that Jordan would get through the airport checks and board his flight home. I sent so much

Reiki that it seemed to be flowing out of every pore of my body. I got so hot I couldn't sleep and spent the night tossing and turning, throwing the covers off and then pulling them back on again.

The next day I went to the airport to pick him up. I hadn't heard from him so was hoping and praying that everything went well and he got his flight. After a very anxious hour or so at Heathrow his flight landed and, still unsure whether he was on it or not, I stood by the barrier in the Arrivals Hall. After what seemed like eleventy billion hours he came through the automatic doors and a big grin spread all over his face when he saw me. I could relax, my boy was home.

Later I asked him how it all went at the airport.

"It was really quite strange," he said. "All their systems went down so they couldn't check in any of the passengers in the usual way and had to do it manually. They had a quick look at my passport, gave me a hand-written boarding pass and let me through."

Oh, the power of Reiki, eh?

So Much Power

After sending Reiki to the situation at the Brazilian airport I began to realise the potential of all that was available to us. I did Reiki and that alone carried an enormous amount of energy and power that could achieve such amazing results. I mean, just imagine sending this energy to anyone, any place, any time, any situation, anywhere in the world and achieve a fantastic result.

No of course I don't know whether my sending Reiki to the Brazilian airport made their systems crash which allowed Jordan to board his flight unhindered, but I'm sure it helped. But from that I began to realise just how much power we all have at our disposal and, as long as it's used for the highest good, it can be extremely helpful in a variety of ways.

If we just take Reiki as one example, yes, it's a healing system that we can use for ourselves and others to bring our bodies back to a state of balance and well-being. But did you also realise that you can send Reiki to help with a situation, as I did with the airport. You can also send distance Reiki to anyone, in any place and at any time, you don't have to be physically present with the recipient for them to benefit. You can send Reiki to help heal any past situation that is still causing you, or someone you know, issues. You can use Reiki to heal past lives that continue to affect someone in this life. You can send Reiki to the future to help with things like upcoming medical appointments, interviews, exams, etc. So just one system and so many uses.

We all know that the power of the mind is huge and can and does affect us physically. We can learn to harness that power for our own good and can potentially change our lives, health and wellbeing. With thought alone with can change our genes and ultimately our health. I used techniques from Joe Dispenza's book *You Are the Placebo Effect* during my recent breast cancer diagnosis, and after surgery am now cancer free with no follow-on treatments or medication.

There's a whole host of therapies and treatments available that have an enormous amount of potential for the individual. Simply set your intention and ask that the right people, the right books, the right courses, and the right way forward shows up for you.

The power is at your fingertips, it's just waiting to be unlocked.

But what if I fail?
Oh but my darling, what if you fly?

Erin Hanson

The Dream

With Jordan safely home and sleeping in his own bed under my roof once again I felt I could relax and focus a little more on my own life and what I wanted to do next. My own Reiki Therapy practice wasn't really taking off but the Reiki Share and our private Spiritual Development Groups were going really well. Maybe that's where my focus should be!

Then I had a dream.

I've never really paid too much attention to dreams before, some are nice and some not so nice but I've never thought too deeply about their meaning. I don't think I dream that much to be honest or if I do I certainly don't remember many of them. I do know that sometimes our guides and angels work with us in a dream state and I'm sure this is what happened with this particular dream. I still remember it to this day so it must have been significant.

In the dream, I had nipped down to my local Sainsbury to get a few bits and pieces but when I came out I couldn't remember where I'd parked my car. The car park was half empty but I still couldn't see it. I used the remote to unlock the doors thinking that I would see the lights and hear it click open. I heard the click and saw the lights flicker out of the corner of my eye, but when I turned towards it I still couldn't see the car. I repeated it a couple of times, heard the click and saw the lights at the periphery of my vision but as I turned towards it, still no car.

I walked back towards the shop and then I found myself on a building site. I knew I couldn't ask the builders about my car as they would laugh and say, "silly bloody woman". As I walked along the building site changed into a beautiful little alleyway, the type you see in lovely Mediterranean villages. It could have been Greek, Italian or even Spanish, I just don't know.

Then I found myself in the home of a middle-aged couple who smiled in welcome but could speak no English. I tried to apologise for suddenly appearing in their home but I don't think they understood, they just kept smiling and welcoming me. I tried to find my way back out of the room, the man opened a door and pointed upwards. There was the biggest step I'd ever seen, it reached up to my waist and I knew I would not be able to get out that way. The man went to another door and, although I couldn't understand what he was saying to the woman, I knew he went to get me a ladder to climb up on. The lady told him not to, that I had to get out by myself. I looked back inside the doorway and at shoulder level I saw two rope handles, one each side of the door. I grabbed hold of the handles and eventually managed to pull myself up onto the step. Once there I could see the way out but it was through a short narrow tunnel; there was bright light at the end. I pushed and shoved and squeezed myself through and as I did so I somehow managed to turn to the woman and said: "it's a bit like giving birth". She simply smiled at me and encouraged me to keep going.

Eventually I came out of the tunnel and just lay on the ground, feeling exhausted.

Then I woke up.

It was all a bit surreal and jumbled as only dreams can be. But when I began to think about it the following morning I began to make sense of it. Losing the car is unlike me as I usually remember roughly where I've parked it, but this I assume to mean that I had started to develop spiritually and then stopped – I had something and then I lost it. Using the remote and seeing the lights is rather like the feeling I sometimes have that I know something amazing, a bit like a eureka moment, but then it slips through my fingers and I've lost it and I can't bring it back.

I'm not quite sure of the significance of the Mediterranean village home but the couple seemed to be expecting me – I think they were sent to help and encourage me on my journey. We couldn't communicate but we understood one another – you don't always need words to communicate. The man clearly wanted to help but the lady seemed to know that I had to achieve it on my own – find my own way. It wasn't easy to get through the doorway, I struggled to get up the step and big steps are always murder on my knees, but then I did have help with the rope handles.

Now at that time I'd been questioning long and hard especially where my Reiki work was concerned. Was I cut out for that kind of work, was all my spirituality real or just a figment of my imagination, could I trust enough to go with the flow? My thoughts went on and on for quite a while.

But now the dream seemed to be telling me that yes, it's hard sometimes but if you put the effort in you will achieve your aims. The struggle through the tunnel bit was me being reborn, finally breaking through and making that connection within myself and realising that I am exactly where I should be.

Now you may say it was just a dream, or you may give me a completely different interpretation, but I am very happy with my version.

Guided by Spirit

When I realised, many years ago, that I had spirit guides and they were here to help and guide me through life I thought how wonderful that was and that they would tell me what to do next! Ha – it doesn't work like that at all!

Yes, we all have guides and angels and many other energy beings that are here to help and guide us, but we simply can't give over responsibility to them and expect our life to run smoothly and to be filled with everything we want. We have to take responsibility for our own lives and take the good with the bad, the rough with the smooth. After all, that's the only way we are going to learn. You watch a baby taking his first steps, he will fall down many times but he doesn't think sod that and never try again. No, he pushes on and one day he is walking firm and steady. He's mastered the rough bits, got through the falls and tumbles and has emerged victorious.

That's life – full of tumbles and falls and we have to find our way through. But in finding our way through we are guided by spirit. However, we have to listen and interpret what they are telling us. And that's not easy.

Meditation is the best and simplest way to listen. Yes, I know, you may find it difficult, and you may have tried it once or twice and thought you couldn't do it so gave up. But there are many ways to meditate, it's not a one size fits all. Meditation is a practice, the more you do it the easier it becomes. When I sit to meditate I first set my intent, I ask my question and then I wait. My answers come in thought form.

Sometimes our guides will communicate with us in dreams, as mine did in the previous chapter. It's not always easy to understand the meaning, but write the dream down and sit with it for a while and the meaning will start to come.

Listen to your own body and your gut feeling. Maybe your guides are making you feel this way because something is not quite right and you need to be aware of it. Work with that feeling, when do you get it, when is it at its strongest, what makes it go away?

Can you imagine how frustrated our guides must get when they're frantically trying to tell us something and we're simply not listening?

Of course, at the end of the day, we still have our own free will and we get to decide what direction our lives go in. If we sit back and do nothing, nothing will change. If we're willing to take the bull by the horns and have a go then something will surely happen. Yes, we may fall flat on our face so much better to listen to some guidance before we proceed.

Teaching Reiki

Over the years, I have taught Reiki to many people, but I will always remember my first time – well you do, don't you?

Gill had asked me to attune her to Reiki Level III and I agreed. Now I can hear some Reiki Masters drawing their breath through pursed lips at my going straight into teaching Level 3, rather than starting at the beginning but you should know by now that I don't faff about too much, I just dive straight in head first. Not always the best thing to do, but hey that's me!

In my defence, I will just say that Gill was already a really good friend and I knew that she was more than ready for this attunement. She is passionate about her Reiki work and takes the responsibility of becoming a Reiki Master seriously. I asked my guides if it was the right thing to do and they gave their blessing. I followed my own intuition and everything was sitting well with me.

The date had been in my diary for two to three weeks and I had prepared as well as I knew how. The manuals were written and I had rehearsed giving an attunement many times. I started talking to my guides about the day and asked for their help for my personal preparation. The night before was a sleepless one and I was glad when it was time to get up! In the shower I was nattering away to my "people", asking for help, asking them to make it alright and asking them to make it good for Gill. Ask, ask, ask, ask, ask – they must really be getting fed up with my constant asking. Out of the shower and I turned the radio on and what was the first song I heard? George Michael singing "you've gotta have faith"! A huge smile broke out, yes, they were doing this with me.

Gill and I started and it just flowed – we didn't always keep to the programme, but it didn't matter. This was Gill's training, Gill's attunement, and it would be right for her. We did a fantastic meditation. Then it was time for the attunement and, I have to be totally honest here, there was a moment when I couldn't think and I did panic a bit. Then I relaxed and said "help". They took over and guided me through the rest of it. The attunement was done and I couldn't get a word out of Gill. She finally said "wow" a couple of times and eventually she could tell me of her experience. I won't share that with you because it was Gill's experience, her story to tell if she chooses to, but suffice it to say I think she had an amazing attunement.

Personally, I thought I could have done better and I am almost certain that I missed something out. But I was told that I did ok, and that the intent was the crucial thing and I had set my intent at the beginning.

After lunch we got down to some practical work. Gill gave me a Reiki session using her new Master symbol. Wow, another truly amazing experience. Again, I can only talk from my experience, but it was the first time that I felt the energy really work its way through my entire body. I was aware of each spinning chakra and saw each colour. The feeling of unconditional love was overwhelming and, yes, the tears were flowing.

So my first teaching experience was absolutely amazing. It felt so right and I knew that I wanted to do more of that.

I have to thank Gill for being my first student, but then someone had to be first!!

A Sudden Passing

I heard of a young woman who passed suddenly. Everyone who knew her and her family were in a state of shock and wondering why life was so cruel.

It made me think about my own feelings and, I must admit, I found I was questioning too. But I had my thoughts which I will share with you now.

I was very sorry that the young woman had passed, but her time here was over. She had chosen her life before coming here, had completed what she came here to do and it was time for her to go. I knew that she was going home and would be looked after during her transition; she would be ok.

My thoughts and love went to her family and friends who were struggling to come to terms with their loss, and trying to find answers why it had to happen. But it doesn't make it any less painful to deal with the physical loss of a loved one from this life, even for those who have the answers.

But they, too, had chosen their life and maybe the loss was one of their lessons, maybe some of them had to learn to deal with loss and grief. I didn't know, but they were my thoughts at the time and they are still my thoughts now.

But, surprisingly, what I found during that time was that the knowledge I had did not make it any easier for me, in fact if anything it made it harder. Whilst everyone else was ranting and raving about the injustice, the tragedy, how could God be so cruel, etc, I found that I couldn't join them because I knew different. They thought I was hard and uncaring.

At that time, I couldn't tell them my truth – for one they wouldn't have believed me and secondly, I didn't think it was my place to do so.

All I can do when anyone passes is to make Reiki available for anyone who wishes to accept it and hold the space for them to heal.

What Next?

So, there I was plodding my way through life. I left my job at the Care Home to concentrate on my Reiki business but, to be honest, it was not working out the way I imagined it would, which was yet another lesson. We try so hard to control our life and manipulate it into the way we want it to be rather than letting go and allowing life to flow. We expect our life to turn out exactly how we want and the trouble with that is the constant disappointment when reality doesn't live up to expectation. Yes, we can have dreams and ambitions and even goals to reach, but we need to get out of our own way at times to allow what's meant for us to flow.

Once I finally stopped trying to force something that wasn't meant for me, my life started to change and for the better.

Our Reiki Shares and Spiritual Development Groups were going really well and it started Gill and I wondering what else might be possible. There was a lack of this type of spiritual practice in our area so maybe there was a gap in the market so to speak.

I should add here that both Gill and I are very grounded, down-to-earth women who have a total love for life and want to enjoy it to the full. We both have an over-developed sense of humour and can burst into uncontrollable fits of laughter just by looking at each other. We love to party and we love a drink. We somehow manage to bring out the positive in every situation and inject some much-needed humour when the going gets tough.

Having said that, we can both empathise with others when facing a tough time. Gill was a Holistic Therapist and was very much into the hands-on approach and could bring a great deal of relief and comfort to those in need. I, on the other hand, was more into the listening type of work and just letting people 'get it off their chest'. My hands-on work was limited to Reiki and even there I worked mainly hands off! It's not that I don't like touching people, I do and I definitely love a hug, but I seemed to get as much, if not more, with the hands off approach.

So here we were, both of us Reiki Master Teachers with a wealth of spiritual experience between us – was it now time to start helping others who were embarking on the whole mind, body and spirit journey?

We started fairly small with a few meditation groups and talks. One of the founders of our Reiki Share Group, Jackie, was developing her passion for crystals so we did a session with her. She did a talk on the properties of various crystals and how to use them and she followed that up with a practical demonstration. Jackie went on to hone her knowledge and skills in the use of crystals and now runs her own business called *Crystaljak*.

We organised a talk on Indigo Children and ran a Spiritual Fayre. All were well attended and Gill and I really felt we had the beginnings of something worthwhile, so we formed our own little business and we called it Como Centre for Enlightenment – Como for the first two letters of our surnames.

I placed my trust in my "people" and asked for help on how to get Como off the ground. We needed a launch event of some sort but had no idea what we could do – they did! They put the idea in my head and, oh boy, was it a good one. But I was unsure whether it would happen and was hesitant about making that first approach. But they had given me this idea so the very least I could do was to try – I made the first approach.

Dominic C. James is a Reiki Master and author of The Reiki Man trilogy and he lived in our area. I needed to contact him and ask if he would be willing to be our Guest Speaker at our launch event. I sent an e-mail.

As soon as I hit that send button my brain kicked in with "it will never happen", "he'll charge too much", "he'll say no" and on and on it went. I checked my e-mails every 5-minutes for a week – no reply. That's it, he wouldn't do it, he didn't want to know – Gill and I would have to come up with another plan for our launch. Later I was mulling over what kind of event we could come up with and what a shame that Dominic didn't want to do it as he would have been so perfect. I was still very much focussed on Dominic doing the event and wondered if someone "upstairs" could give him a bit of a nudge.

An hour later I had an e-mail from Dominic – yes, he would do it!!!!! I was overjoyed and once again my people had come up trumps. But I had forgotten that Dominic was a Reiki Master too and a very spiritual person – it's in our make-up to help when we can.

I was excited about launching our Centre and all the wonderful things we could do and the journeys that we will be undertaking. I was excited about meeting our guest speaker and hearing of his journey into Reiki and how he became an author. I was looking forward to meeting lots of new people. I was excited about helping people who were keen to start or move on with their spiritual journey.

But I was nervous that the evening would be a disaster and that Dominic might think it had all been a waste of his time. I was nervous in case nobody turned up. I was also nervous about the huge leap into the unknown.

But I needn't have worried because the whole evening was a success, people turned up and Dominic was lovely. I floated around on a high all evening and I loved every minute of being in a hall full of like-minded people who chatted, asked questions and showed genuine enthusiasm for our new venture.

On Friday 15 June 2011, we launched our new venture and the Como Centre was born.

Two Sides of Me

Many years ago, when my spiritual development got going, I was eager to share and talk to anyone who would listen about my beliefs and values. Possibly over-enthusiastic, and definitely naïve, I was once called "The Daughter of the Devil" by a Methodist church goer who was totally horrified by my beliefs and practices.

I never thought that my beliefs were bad or harmful to anyone and, of course, they were not. I had just started my journey of discovery and I was keen and eager to learn. She never asked me what my beliefs were, but when I mentioned that I went to a Spiritualist Church she went ballistic. Quite embarrassing really because I was running a slimming club at the time and her display was very public. I remember being totally shocked because, although I knew that we probably held different views, I really thought tolerance and acceptance of others were good traits to have in all religions.

That day I learnt then to keep my beliefs to myself and I never discussed my thoughts with anyone who was not of a similar mind. Of course, along the way I met some wonderful people who I could share and discuss with and learn from but, overall, I kept my spiritual side separate and private.

Most of my friends and family know the side of me that is very down to earth, loves a good time and enjoys life. They may possibly be very surprised to learn of the other me but I hope they understand that my spirituality is very important. They can be totally reassured, however, that the down-to-earth me will not disappear – I am still up for a good time!

There is another group who knows my spiritual side but are not too familiar with the down-to-earth side. I hope that they are not too shocked when they get to know the other me!

The third group, and the smallest group, know the complete me. Most of this group are of a similar mind (or at least have an open mind) and are always keen to enter lively discussions and share views and beliefs. They accept the whole me for who I am and do not want to change me.

But since my involvement with Reiki I found that my spiritual development was growing by leaps and bounds and keeping the two different sides of me separate was causing conflict within. I am who I am, both sides make the whole - it was time to allow them to merge and become one.

Yes, I lost a few friends along the way. There were those who thought I'd lost the plot completely. But I've come to understand that people come and go throughout life, those who are meant to be with you will stay and others are just passing through, possibly just to teach you something.

I totally accept the whole person that I am. One day I could be sitting outside in nature in deep meditation and connecting with all sorts of beings, the next I could be out partying and enjoying a drink or three with a group of friends.

As the song goes … This Is Me!

After the High ...

After floating around on a bit of a high on the Saturday after the launch of Como, I came crashing back down on Sunday.

I had a phone call to tell me that my father had a stroke! He was 87-years old and lived alone but amazingly he happened to be with a neighbour when it happened. The neighbour called an ambulance and Dad was taken straight to hospital. I rushed to be there, but the two-and-a-half-hour drive seemed to take forever. When I got to the hospital he was conscious but paralysed down the right side of his body and had lost his speech.

I felt totally useless and out of control, all I could do was pump tons of Reiki into him and boy, was he drawing it.

Over the next few days I was constantly being told that it was still too early to think about the long-term prognosis but, for him, the stroke was the worst possible thing that could have happened and I wasn't sure how he would cope. He was a very independent, proud man and the limits his age placed on his body already frustrated him.

The following week was one of highs and lows. There were several times when we thought "this is it", but he hung on in there. There was one day that was the best I'd seen him all week and I thought all would be well. We were not out of the woods though and would just have to wait and to see.

I wasn't sure of my own feelings at that time. Part of me wanted him to pass to a better life because I certainly didn't want him to have to live with paralysis and being tube fed. He couldn't talk either which was hard for him because he was a talker and a great teller of tales. But I didn't want to lose my Dad.

Worrying would not change a thing. I tried to live in the present moment but it was hard. We all have to lose people we love and all I wanted the best for my Dad, but I couldn't make it happen the way I wanted it to be.

But it was his journey to make and, although I was with him as much as I possibly could, this was one journey that I couldn't make with him.

A week on and there was no improvement at all and during one visit the doctor called me aside and told me that Dad's body was beginning to shut down and I should prepare for the worst.

It's funny you know, although I've always known about the bigger picture, I think I am now beginning to realise that it is so. Dad's stroke, whilst horrendous for him and for us in this lifetime, it is but a fraction of the lifetimes that have gone and of those to come. It's like I am getting little glimpses of the whole and then I snap back into now – does that make sense? It's quite difficult to explain but I'm sure you'll know what I'm talking about.

While my Dad's stroke was horrible for all of us, I was mindful that we were not the only family going through it. There was a whole building, at just that one hospital, of families who were and still are coping in the best way they can.

Dad finally passed the following week and went home.

Throughout my lifetime I have said goodbye to many people who I have loved, but it's hard to say goodbye to a parent. My Dad had always been there for me, through the good times and the tough times, and I would miss not having him around to share my life with. But I was not totally consumed by grief – I was terribly, terribly sad, yes, but I was ok. I was just eighteen when my Mum passed and I remember that feeling of all-consuming despair, the grief because I would never see her again, the anger that she had been taken from me and, yes, the need to blame someone for her death.

Forty years on and I felt totally different. Was it because I was older and wiser? Was it because my Dad was older and had a good life? Was it because at the age of 87 he was nearing his time to go? Well, yes, it could be any one or a combination of those things, but more importantly I knew now that his passing was not the end of my Dad.

Through this whole period of Dad's illness and his passing I learnt some valuable lessons. I learnt that I don't always have to be strong for others, so now if I want to cry I will. Grief is an emotion to be experienced and owned, soon it will start to subside.

I have learned not to feel guilty about things that are outside of my control. I could not have been with Dad as he passed because he deteriorated too rapidly to allow me to make the 2-hour journey to be with him.

I will not allow others to make me question myself as to whether I could have/should have done more. I did what I could at the time and with the knowledge I had so I will not live with regrets.

I guess when anyone passes, the past and the memories are at the forefront of the mind. My memories are, on the whole, happy and loving ones. Yes, there are a few that could have been better but who wouldn't change a few things if it were possible? What I found was that when the not so good memories cropped up I was somehow able to make peace with them and then let them go. As well as having to clear my Dad's home, I also had a good old clear out of all the clutter that I was holding inside and I let go of a lot of things that no longer served me.

So, with everything completed, I was left to adjust to a life without my Dad. And yet I know he's still with me.

Gratitude

Several years ago, I was inspired by a friend to keep a Gratitude Diary for a year. In Reiki and spiritual development, we are encouraged to be grateful for our many blessings in life and, indeed, there are many things in this life that I am extremely grateful for. But could I find something for 365/6 days?

The answer, at that time, was I honestly didn't know.

Every day I woke up wondering what my blessing would be that day. Sometimes it was so obvious it smacked me right in the face. Other days I would drift into the evening and nothing was forthcoming. Those non-forthcoming days were usually the ones I spent at home, having little interaction with the outside world and few opportunities for spur-of-the-moment happenings.

It's those days where I would start to reflect and think a little deeper about all sorts of things. I would often sit gazing out of the window and wait for a bit of inspiration, but I was seeing the garden full of shrubs, trees and wildlife, and started to wonder how often I appreciated the beauty of it all? I would read a book, but not give a thought about the complexities of the eyes and the ability to read the written word? I would listen to the conversation around me, but how often did I really hear what was being said? How often did I sit and lose myself in music rather than just have it playing in the background?

I realised then there was so much in life to be grateful for if only we stopped and thought about it.

My "blessings" were many and varied over that year. Some were really simple, and some may think they're not a blessing at all, but finding a dress for £3 in the Marks and Spencer sale really gave me pleasure! Others were bigger blessings and more thought provoking.

At the time, I didn't think I would keep my Gratitude Diary going for longer than a couple of weeks, let alone a month. I had tried keeping diaries many times before and although the idea appeals greatly, the practical side always let me down.

I decided to take to social media with daily postings of my gratitude. I reasoned that if I was held accountable to someone or something, then I might just succeed. So, I posted every day and discovered that by the end of the year I was finding stuff to be grateful for everywhere. It changed me and I was finding joy in so many things that I simply took for granted.

It's true what they say – 'the more you're grateful for, the more you have to be grateful for'.

The Power of Reiki

Although I started this new phase of my life with Reiki I had, over the past few years, branched out to include a few new things and tried to incorporate all my spirituality into my new venture with Gill and Como. But Reiki will always continue to surprise and amaze me with its power.

There was one time that will always stay in my memory. Gill had sent me a text to say that a little boy we both knew from the Children's Clinic was very ill in hospital and could I join her in sending Reiki. He was on a ventilator and in the High Dependency Unit, it was not looking good.

All day long we sent Reiki but by late afternoon we both decided that, if the parents agreed, we would visit that evening and give a little more Reiki directly to him.

When we arrived at the hospital we found that he was off the ventilator and had been moved onto a ward. Things were looking better but his heart rate was still very high. The nurses were not too keen to let us in, but the parents insisted. Gill and I took a side of the bed each and started to give Reiki. After a while Gill nodded to me and turned her eyes towards the monitors - his heart rate was beginning to drop. I stood by the monitor, still pumping Reiki, and watching this child's heart rate slowly start to drop. By the time we left the hospital it was almost back to normal.

His parents were absolutely delighted and relieved that their little boy was showing all the signs of making a good recovery. The nursing staff, although a little surprised at how rapidly his heart rate returned to normal, took it all in their stride and were completely unaware that he had been receiving Reiki.

If I had not seen that heart monitor with my own eyes I would have found it hard to believe that there was such a rapid improvement. Oh I knew that Reiki worked, I had no doubt about that, but in the space of around 15-20 minutes the child's heart rate was almost back to normal! Absolutely amazing and a real privilege to be able to help this little boy and his parents.

Not all parents are aware of, or have access to, Reiki. Many medics would say that Reiki makes no difference whatsoever and its only conventional medicine that works. But how marvellous would it be if patients were offered Reiki alongside conventional medicine?

Now I know the sceptics out there would say that this little boy would probably have improved anyway, and maybe he would – who knows. But if it was your child, what would you do?

Life Lessons

Over my lifetime, I have seen many atrocities committed against humanity and some of them in the name of religion. I remember one incident where a pupil killed one of his schoolteachers. The nation was horrified, and quite rightly so. What on earth was our world coming to when a young person could take another's life so carelessly. I thought about this tragic incident for a long while, trying to understand and make sense of it all.

I had learned that, on a spiritual level, before his birth the boy would have chosen those actions as his life lesson to learn. Coming from the same Soul Group the teacher agreed to play her part in his lesson and chose to be the victim. From the teacher's point of view her job was done, she had helped the young man and could go home. The boy had to continue with his lesson and live out the rest of his life coping with the tough consequences. From a spiritual perspective, this all sounds logical and quite simple, but from our limited life experience, our own reality, this is just appalling and tragic. So, what was his lesson to learn, you may ask? I have no idea and I shouldn't think he did either – in this lifetime.

Now don't get me wrong, just because I understood all that on a spiritual level doesn't mean that I like it. I felt a deep sadness for the teacher and her family and I also felt compassion for the boy and his family - they were all going through a very tough time.

I live in this world where acts of violence appal and anger me; the blatant disregard some folk have for others is shocking to say the least. Sometimes I want to hit out and retaliate, but that's not the answer. As Gandhi once said, *an eye for an eye makes the whole world blind.*

I didn't have the answers then and I still don't have any now, maybe there are none. Maybe this is exactly how it's meant to be until we all start to realise that humanity must change, that we have to move, as one, towards love and compassion in order to survive.

I remember someone once told me that the spiritual path is a tough one and as soon as we get a little clarity in one area, then a whole load more questions start to rise to the surface and so the whole quest for answers begins again.

I will never ever regret choosing the spiritual path. It has awakened my awareness of belonging to something far greater than just living my life on earth. There is so much more that we are a part of. It's a bit like just discovering you have an extended family that you were unaware of and slowly getting to know each of them, their lives and how they entwine with yours.

My life feels more complete even though I have more questions than answers.

Premises

After the launch of Como in June our work was really starting to take off. Events were successful and people were asking to join some of our groups. We were beginning to get noticed.

We were still working out of our local village hall, which was fine in many respects but certainly had its drawbacks. The main one being that we were amassing more and more stuff with nowhere to store it. Every time we met we'd spend half an hour or so setting up and then another half an hour packing everything away at the end of the evening.

Gill and I started to think about how nice it would be to have a space of our own where we could set everything up and leave it. We'd sit and dream of somewhere local, safe, warm and dry and above all inexpensive. Not too much to ask then! We didn't know it then but we had set our intention in motion.

It was around November time that Gill and I went into our bank to sort out a bank account. We didn't have any money but I had an old account which I hadn't used for years. It had about £40 in it so I thought we could simply use that for any Como money, but Gill needed to be added to the account.

When we'd finished, and left the bank, Gill turned to me and said, "we need to go in there", pointing to the estate agents across the road.

"What? Are you mad? We haven't got any money".

"Humour me", she replied, as she set off across the street.

We went but just looking at the properties on display in the window it soon became clear that we couldn't afford anything on offer. We were so disappointed, her more so than me I think as she was convinced there would be something there for us. Just as we were about to leave one of the sales agents came over to us.

"What exactly are you two ladies looking for?", he asked. We told him we wanted somewhere local to rent, a couple of rooms or just a big space, and not too expensive.

"Hang on a minute" he said, and disappeared out to a back office. He came back a couple of minutes later clutching some details that he thought might just interest us.

"This might be just what you're looking for," he said, and handed us a couple of leaflets.

We took the details and went back to Gill's house. We made a cup of tea and then poured over the leaflets. It looked good on paper but we needed to look. We didn't have any money but that didn't stop us from taking the next step. I phoned the estate agent and managed to get an appointment to view that afternoon.

We were getting excited but we tried to reign it in because it might turn out not to be suitable at all, and money was in short supply. The space available was just one huge room, with windows on two sides which let in so much light, shared use of a small kitchen and toilets, and plenty of parking. We left that building even more excited than when we walked in.

We went back to Gill's and talked about it for ages – should we, shouldn't we. We both wanted to do it very much but we felt there was a need to be sensible, after all we had no money and we needed to pay a year's rent up front. We decided to sleep on it.

I went home and talked it over with Pat. She was unsure about the whole thing but she could see how much it meant to me to be doing what I loved with no restrictions. She offered to lend us the rent! Bloody hell, I have the most amazing people in my life. There were of course conditions attached, one of which was to see if we could pay the rent 6-monthly rather than annually and she made me promise that if we couldn't make a go of the business in the first year then we would give up the premises.

I phoned Gill. Nothing had changed with her overnight and we both still had this overwhelming urge to go with it. Financially it was a bit of a risk, but if we didn't try we would never know.

We phoned the estate agent and the deal was done. We moved into our new Como home the following January.

I really felt that we were guided all the way - everything went so smoothly. We were so grateful for all the help that we were given from our Guides, the Universe and Pat.

We worked hard and by the end of the first year we had enough money to pay Pat back what she leant us and also the following year's rent.

We turned the room into a lovely space that had the most wonderful calming atmosphere. We spent the following 10-years doing some fabulous work and we met many wonderful people, some fairly weird ones too. Above all we had so much fun, so many laughs and Gill and I were very happy there.

So, if you have a dream, ask the Universe to help you. You may not get it tomorrow but, if it's in your best interests, you will get all the help you need. Remember though, you do have to act upon the guidance you're given!

Synchronicity is an ever present reality
for those who have eyes to see.

Carl Jung

Lights in the Sky

Over the years of my spiritual development I have learnt to question everything. I can't believe something someone else tells me just because it's right for them. My questioning can lead to some excellent conversations with others and with myself. More often than not one simple question will give rise to umpteen more, but isn't that the way it should be? Just listen to children, the constant "why" that came from my son when he was little sometimes drove me mad, but that's the way they learn.

Years ago, I saw a very bright light in the sky and I remember it quite well. It dropped rapidly behind the rooftops and I lost sight of it and ten minutes later it re-appeared and whizzed around the sky for at least 10-15 minutes. I didn't think it was an aircraft, it was completely silent and I had never seen anything like it before. Whatever was it?

Not surprisingly I thought of UFOs and aliens and then my thoughts started to drift.

Our minds are naturally programmed to find the most logical explanation for what our eyes are seeing and yet, when there is no logical explanation, some still cannot believe alternative options.

Why couldn't those lights have been from a UFO? Because we have never had any known encounters with aliens before? Because aliens are just the subject of Sci-Fi books and films?

Now there are lots of things that happen in life that, whilst perfectly normal to me, are deemed as complete chance or coincidence by others. Personally, I think it's a little naïve of us to think that we are the only life force in the Universe. Just because we have never seen it doesn't mean it doesn't exist. I've never seen the Northern Lights but I know they exist.

I have a completely open mind, anything is possible until proven to me one way or the other. Therefore, aliens could exist and they may well be highly intelligent beings. They could be of enormous help to us, they could teach us all sorts of things, we could build a mutually beneficial relationship. But what scares me is that if aliens do exist, and they have the capability of visiting earth, would the powers that be automatically go on the attack and ruin any chances that we may have of opening a dialogue? Would an alien race be accepted when our world has such deep problems with racism? Would we accept aliens who do not look, and think, like we do when we are so quick to judge those who don't conform to our way of thinking?

At the end of the day these are just my thoughts and you will have your own. Sometimes it's only when we have an "experience" that we start to think more deeply and question what we are seeing and feeling. There is so much in this great Universe of ours that we don't know about or understand, and the future could be so exciting if only we could set aside our pre-conceived ideas and fears.

But all of that didn't answer my question – what were those lights in the sky?

Training

Just before we moved into our premises it became clear that we needed to turn our focus to training of some sort. It was all very well holding a few events and Reiki Share Groups but that was never going to bring in enough money to pay the rent.

Gill was a holistic therapist and had many years' experience in that field. She already held her teaching certificate so suggested we try to get some of the holistic courses accredited and teach them. We started writing manuals in November knowing that the sooner we got on with it the sooner we could start earning the rent money. Gill wanted to get accreditation through the Guild of Beauty and Holistic Therapists and that was fine by me. They agreed to take a look at our manuals but warned that accreditation would take around 3-4 months to come through, added to that that Christmas and the New Year holidays were not that far away so could take longer.

We worked really hard with the manuals – Gill writing and me editing. By the beginning of December, we submitted our first ten manuals and waited on tenterhooks for either the rejection or the corrections to be made.

We needn't have worried because by the end of December we had all ten of our manuals accredited. We were ready to teach.

At that time, all I had to contribute was Reiki, which was clearly not enough. The first thing I needed to do was get my teacher training certificate, or PTLLS as it was called then. I did it on-line and by assignment but I had to go to Oxford for my teaching practical. I didn't enjoy the course much, but I learnt a lot and it was a means to an end. I eventually passed and got my certificate.

My next course, and I have to say one of the best for me personally and for Como, was the Meditation Teacher one. It was both theory and practical and again, I learnt a lot plus this time I loved the course. When I gained my certificate, I started teaching Meditation at Como and we held regular meditation groups.

And so my training continued, sometimes on-line courses and sometimes I would go off for training. Sometimes Gill and I did a course together, and other courses I did alone. Some of the courses I loved and others not so much but Gill and I were having the best time ever and the knowledge we gained from each course we used in Como. We both agreed that it was an absolute waste to have knowledge and not pass it on to others. We wrote course after course and workshop after workshop, offering our students a wide range of subjects to study.

I've lost count of the number, and subjects, of courses I took and to this day I still have that thirst for learning. I look at courses on offer and think 'oooo that might be useful, or that might be a great subject to learn'. You never stop learning though, whether it be through training courses or by life experiences. There is so much out there and we almost owe it to ourselves to take full advantage of it to expand our own minds.

Gill and Me

Gill and I were beginning to spend a lot of time together. Before we had our premises, we would get together, usually down the pub, and talk about what we wanted to do next. Once we had found Como then we had a base and spent a lot of time there, either getting it the way we wanted it or delivering training courses together. Our friendship was growing nicely.

We had both been warned by other people that starting a business with someone you barely knew was extremely risky. Others had told us that developing a friendship after becoming business partners was the best way to go. It didn't matter to us how our friendship came about, what mattered was that it was a good one and it was growing daily.

We were discovering things about each other all the time. I discovered that Gill is a bit of a perfectionist, she likes everything to be in the right place and if something doesn't feel right she'll move it. She was constantly moving the furniture about at Como. She will always have the final word and she'll argue black and blue to stand by what she believes. Once she gets angry over something, or someone pisses her off, she's like a Rottweiler on heat. She's a Scorpio and once the tail comes up it could stay up for days. I've witnessed her having a go at someone and nothing I could ever say would calm her down, she's best left alone for a while when that happens.

Having said all that, there is the other side. She's loving and kind, she's funny and great fun. She has a wicked sense of humour that matches mine and we can go into fits of uncontrollable laughter just by looking at each other. She laughs a lot. She's loyal and honest and will tell me if I've stepped out of line or pissed her off in some way. She's great fun to work with, there is always laughter in any of our courses or workshops. She's great fun to be on a night out with and rarely says no when I suggest we get another bottle of wine!

Over the years our friendship grew strong enough for her to suggest that we go on holiday together. I was up for that but did have to wonder how well we would get on being together 24/7 for a whole week. Well it would either make or break us that was for sure. We went to Rhodes and I can honestly say we barely stopped laughing from the moment we got picked up to go to the airport till the moment we were dropped off again. We had an amazing time and the memories we made will stay with me forever. We also did a lot of planning around Como and the way we wanted to take our business, and came home with a plan of action.

We had planned another holiday for the following year, this time creating havoc in Croatia, but Covid put a stop to that. As soon as some kind of normal returns and we can travel again, you can bet your life that we'll turn up in some place or other and cause a bit of a stir!

Jerry

We hadn't been in our new premises too long before we became aware of some really weird bangs and crashes and other strange happenings that we didn't have a logical explanation for, and usually happening when we were alone in the building.

I should just explain that our space was above a garage showroom and we occupied half of the first floor. The other half was given over to offices, toilets and a kitchen. Above us was extensive loft space. We got on really well with the guys in the showroom but the women in the offices were a bit standoffish. Although the guys in the showroom worked 7-days a week, they went home around 6pm and the office staff were strictly 9-5, 5-days a week. We had plenty of time on our own in the building.

One particular evening we were clearing up to go home probably around 8pm-ish so not particularly late, but it was winter so it was dark outside. Gill was in the kitchen washing the cups when she suddenly came flying into our room and slammed the door shut behind her. She looked as white as a ghost.

"Whatever's the matter?" I asked.

"There's somebody there", she replied.

"Can't be", I said, "we're alone in the building".

"Somebody stood right behind my right shoulder and whispered 'GILLY' so loud in my right ear".

"Well who?", I asked.

"I don't bloody know, I ran in here!"

Jeez, what was that all about? She was really freaked out about that and wouldn't go in the kitchen on her own again for ages.

The next time we were alone in the building we heard someone walking up the corridor. We went to check but no-one was in the building. Another time we were holding an event so had quite a few people in our room. Everyone could hear the noise coming from the showroom downstairs, it sounded like chairs being scraped along the floor. Gill and I went to check and took one of the men with us, but there was no one there.

A few months went by with similar stuff going on. It started to quieten down when it was Gill and I in the building but really kicked off when other people were with us.

We held an Evening of Mediumship and our room was packed with people, the noises were relentless and everyone was getting a bit spooked. The medium for the evening, who was a good friend of ours, came to us during the break and asked if we were aware of someone in the building who had passed. We were. The owner of the garage had passed away several years earlier and, in fact, our room used to be his office and boardroom. We could often sense him in the room with us and sometimes walking along the corridor.

"No", she said, "this is someone else. A man. He's not happy with people being in his building. He's ok with you two now, but he didn't like it much at the beginning. He'll keep an eye on you though and warn you if he's not happy with the type of people you're bringing in".

Bloody hell! Gill and I looked at each other wide-eyed and mouths open. We have our own resident ghost!

A few days later we were chatting to the managing director and we just asked if there was someone who worked there who had since passed. He told us of Jerry. Jerry was the odd-job man who had a learning difficulty, but he wasn't sure what. He said Jerry could be an awkward sod and either liked you or didn't. If he didn't like you then you knew about it.

Jerry! This was our 'ghost'.

Once we knew about Jerry we got along quite well. He kept up his noise disturbances when there were other people in the building but on the whole, he was fairly quiet with us. He did warn us about people though and a couple of times we got close to trusting someone who wasn't right for us and Jerry made his feelings known, loud and clear.

His most spectacular intervention came just after Gill and I had been chatting about how nice it would be if the girls in the offices along the corridor were relocated to another area on site and we took over the whole of the upstairs. Two days later we went in to find several workmen along the upstairs corridor and down in the showroom. One of the guys told us that the taps in the ladies toilets had been left on overnight and had not only flooded the upstairs corridor but had also seeped into the showroom below. The taps were off when we left the previous evening and the office staff had left long before us. Strangely though, the water never got into our room.

Was Jerry trying to clear the offices for us? We had a word with him, thanked him for trying to help but asked him not to resort to anything quite as drastic again.

How Meditation Can Help

After I had completed my Meditation Teacher Training course we held our first 6-week course teaching others how to meditate. I was both excited and nervous at the prospect, but I know that meditation could be so beneficial in many ways.

I want to share one of my student's stories with you here. I have her permission to do so, but will call her Ann.

When Ann joined our Meditation Course she was suffering from chronic pain and debilitating headaches, she decided to give meditation a try – almost as a last resort. She came into the room just about pain-free but as we started our first 5-minute meditation, focussing on the breath, Ann was on the verge of a panic attack and severe pain kicked in.

I asked her if she would like to go home but she said she wanted to give it another go, so we started our second meditation. This time was a little better – no panic attack, but the pain remained. Still determined to continue we went into the final, guided, meditation of the evening and Ann felt the intensity of her pain fade a little. As she left she said she would be back the following week.

I was at a bit of a loss – I had never had anyone come into any course pain-free but leave with pain. I decided that, if there was no improvement the following week, I would talk it over with my own meditation teacher.

Ann was back the following week and started the session with slight pain. During the first meditation, she felt the pain ebb and flow; the pain lessened with the second meditation. Our third meditation, The Hot Air Balloon, was our breakthrough. Ann loaded all her pain, plus some other problems and anxieties, into the basket and cut the ropes. As she watched the hot air balloon float away, so did her pain. Ann had found a way to start to gain control.

The improvement continued over the following weeks; with each new meditation Ann was beginning to feel more in control and her pain lessened.

By the last night of the course Ann was only suffering pain about once a week - an enormous improvement.

Through meditation Ann had learnt that she was in control and had a valuable tool at her disposal. She continued to meditate daily, and only used medication whenever her pain became too severe.

One Day at a Time

"Let's take it one day at a time" - I used to hate those words. I didn't want to take it one day at a time – I wanted to know what was going to happen, I wanted to plan, I wanted to be in control. I wanted to know what the result would be.

When I had cancer I was constantly being told "let's just take it one day at a time". I wanted to scream and yell at the doctors – why couldn't they answer my questions, why couldn't they tell me I was going to be ok?

The week following Dad's stroke I had those same feelings. The doctors couldn't give me any answers and I couldn't make any plans. I felt out of control and my life was in limbo, exactly the same feelings I had during the cancer.

However, at that point I took the time to really think about the way I was feeling, and why I needed to be in control of everything. I didn't know the answer then and I still don't, but I do know it doesn't have to be that way.

I decided that I should try to live more in the present, be in the now, but it wasn't always easy to do. And, of course, it was easier when my life was running smoothly but as soon as I had issues to deal with, emotions got in the way and that need to be in control started to flood back. But I decided I wouldn't let the feelings of irritation and impatience, and sometimes even fear, to ruin my day or my week or even my life. I would stop and ask myself if there was anything I could do in that present moment to change the situation.

I had to be honest. If the answer was no, then I let it go because there was nothing I could do. If the answer was yes, then I needed to act on it and change whatever I could to ease the angst.

I'm not pretending it was easy but, you know, living in the now actually does work. Why worry about doing something that you can do nothing about. Put it out of your mind until such time that you can do something about it. And actually, what I found was some of the things that I worried about resolved themselves over time without any action from me.

Give it a go, what have you got to lose?

The Poodle and the Pony

Gill and I continued to work well together and bookings were coming in nicely. We weren't snowed under with work but we had enough to keep us busy.

One morning Gill messaged me. *How do you fancy giving some Reiki to a dog?*

Sounded good to me. I had just completed a course on Animal Reiki so this was a perfect fit, not that I wanted the dog to be poorly of course, but that we could be of some help.

Gill picked me up and drove us to the dog's home which was the next town from where we lived. It's always best to treat animals in their own homes whenever possible as they are more at ease before you start.

"What's wrong with the dog?", I asked Gill.

"I don't know", she replied. "All I know is that a woman from the vets called and asked if I could help."

We eventually found the house and the owner let us in. An elderly lady in full, very colourful, make-up and a mass of curls perched high on top of her head. She took us into the lounge to meet the dog – a poodle. Snap! I'd never really bought into the 'owner looks like their dog' saying, but in this case, it was spot on. Minus the make-up, of course.

We sat and the owner called the dog to her and restrained him.

"No, let him go", I said, "he will come if he wants to".

I'm not sure she was too happy with that but when giving Reiki to animals it's the one time they get to make their own decisions. If they want to receive Reiki they will come to you, if they don't then they don't want it and that's exactly how it should be.

The dog was a black Standard Poodle, so quite big. He had moved to stand in the furthest corner away from us, but watching us the whole time. Gill and I both slid to the floor and allowed our Reiki to flow.

"What's the problem we're treating him for?" Gill asked the owner.

"Well, I think it's anxiety", she replied. "He barks at everyone we meet when we go for a walk, he doesn't like people in his house and he doesn't like men." The owner kept talking, she hardly paused for breath. Gill asked her if she would like to go and get on with something else while we worked with her dog but no, she wasn't budging. On and on she went until eventually Gill asked her to shut up, very nicely of course.

The dog didn't look very anxious to me, but then I didn't know him. I certainly wasn't feeling any anxiety coming off him. But we allowed our Reiki to flow and slowly the dog sat down and then lay on a blanket and went to sleep. He looked pretty relaxed.

When we had finished, the owner asked if we would go the following week and give him another treatment.

The following week the dog seemed a little more relaxed, and settled down to sleep almost immediately. The owner had a friend visiting and the chatter was constant. Once again Gill suggested they might like to go to another room for a cup of tea and a chat. No, they were staying put. Our Reiki flowed, the dog seemed fine and neither Gill or I were picking up any signs of anxiety or stress. We asked the owner if the dog had been any different during the week.

"No", she said. "He's still barking at other dogs and people."

"Isn't that normal dog behaviour?" I said to Gill on the way home.

"Yeah, it is", she replied. "To be honest I think it's more of a problem with the owner than the dog."

We went back the following week as requested and this time the dog came straight to us and spent the entire session laying with his body touching ours. This time there were two friends visiting. The owner said they wanted to see what we did and soak up some of the Reiki energy! We did what we had to do and left.

"Bloody hell", said Gill as we drove away, "that's just taking the piss".

We agreed and that was the last time we saw the dog. There was nothing wrong with him at all. We felt he was picking up on her anxiety every time she took him for a walk, the dog was simply going into protective mode. She was the one who needed the treatment, not the dog.

A couple of days after that I got a phone call from Gill one morning.

"Mrs Poodle had just phoned", she said, "would we go and treat her friend's pony?"

"Oh, bloody hell, should we?"

"We should".

So, we went. I hated the thought of leaving any animal that needed a little help. Mrs Poodle had said that the pony was out in the paddock but the owner would put it in the stable. No, no, no – leave it out. There's nothing more dangerous than treating an animal in a confined space when it's frightened and doesn't want to be treated.

It turned out that the pony was anti-social. It didn't mix with the other horses and it didn't like people! Sodding hell, here we go again.

The owner asked if we would like to go into the field. No, best we stay outside the fence and not in his territory. There were two other horses in the field, both came over to us and were friendly. The "problem" pony was at the far side of the field and appeared completely disinterested. We allowed our Reiki to flow for about 20-minutes or so, the two friendly horses loving it. The pony started to look over to where we were, he was certainly aware of the Reiki energy and was watching. Very slowly he started to make his way across to us. There were many stops and starts along the way but he got to a few feet from the fence and looked at us, really looked at us. Eventually he came over and nuzzled at our hands. It was a beautiful moment. The owner came back down to the field and was amazed at the change in him.

Although she was grateful she never asked us to go back and give her pony more Reiki. She clearly saw the benefit so I hope she found someone to treat him on a regular basis. You never know, she might have trained to do Reiki herself.

Cosmic Ordering

It was suggested that we might like to do some sort of event around Cosmic Ordering, the Law of Attraction, Manifestation, or whatever else you want to call it. Noel Edmunds was a great advocate so we thought if it worked for him then it should work for us, let's give it a go.

I looked at one of the websites we often used and lo and behold, up popped Ellen Watts. She had just written her first book, *Cosmic Ordering Made Easier*, and was now available to give talks. She didn't live too far away from us either, so I booked her.

Both Gill and I knew how the Law of Attraction worked but, to be honest, my success with it was sporadic. It would be good to understand it better and to have the opportunity to improve our approach to it. Having said that though, we were both convinced that our Como Centre came about because of an order that we both placed. Cosmic Ordering was a simple concept, ask for what you want and the Universe will deliver, but there was much more to it than that.

Ellen was immediately likeable, very knowledgeable about the subject and very funny. She told us of the many successes she had simply by asking for what she wanted, and she made it very clear that we could all get what we wanted too. But of course, it wasn't as simple as saying something along the lines of 'I want a new dress' and expecting it to come next day delivery. You had to be specific about what you wanted, colour, size, style, etc. After all if you ordered that dress from on on-line store you would have to be specific. You had to believe that you totally deserved to have that dress and you may even have to put a little effort in to get the dress of your dreams, but above all you totally had to believe that it was on its way to you.

We were all so taken with Ellen and the whole concept of Cosmic Ordering that we invited her back to run a workshop for us. And this is where I learnt so much more about placing and receiving my orders.

One of the first things she talked about was how our own limiting beliefs blocked us from receiving orders! Imagine that – I didn't think anything could block wanting and getting something, after all if you want something you want it!

But just think about it for a moment, how many of you want to win the lottery? But how many believe that you will? How many of you believe that you're not worthy of having success, think you're being greedy if you ask for too much, believe you have to work hard to earn money, that there's no such thing as a free lunch? And so, the list goes on. I certainly have all those beliefs, and many more. We are brought up to believe these things by our parents and society and they can and do hold us back from realising our dreams and ambitions.

So the first job is to get rid of those limiting beliefs, and that's not easy.

The second part to Cosmic Ordering is to be specific about what you want. Write down what you really want, be as specific as possible and add a deadline. The Universe can't deliver what it doesn't know you want.

The third part is to add "for the good of all concerned" at the end of every order placed. You don't want to receive something at the misfortune of others or indeed yourself. For example, you wouldn't want to lose a stone in weight by having your leg amputated! Fair point.

Finally, be open to receive your order. Don't think for a minute that it will be as easy as being delivered to your door by Amazon or DHL – you may have to put a little effort in.

We learnt a lot more at that Workshop but those were the basics that I use today when placing an order.

At the morning break, after we had covered those four basic principles Ellen set us the task of placing an order, a surprise gift, to be received by the end of the day, for the good of all concerned.

I placed my order and then forgot all about it as we carried on with the workshop. When I got home that evening Pat said something had arrived for me during the day and gave me a beautiful bouquet of flowers. They were from some friends, not because it was my birthday or any special occasion, but simply because!

Bloody hell, it worked! How wonderful.

But not all my orders went to plan.

Shortly after the workshop I saw an article in a national newspaper asking for people who had retrained or started a new career at or after the age of 60 to e-mail their story. "Oooo, that's me" I thought and spent the next 30-minutes umming and arring about whether I should e-mail or not.

Eventually I sent the e-mail, reasoning that I had been presented with an opportunity and it was down to me to grab it. That evening I placed a cosmic order asking that I would be successful and my story would be featured, for the good of all concerned. The following day an e-mail came back saying that my story had been submitted to the Editor for consideration. I put the whole thing out of my mind.

A couple of days later and another e-mail - the Editor thought my story was fascinating and wanted to feature it. I was asked if I could do a telephone interview the following day and whether I would be available for a photo shoot on the Friday! Excited was an understatement.

The interview went well and at the end of the week I went off to the Centre to meet the photographer and a stylist - yes, I was getting a make-over too. Well how fabulous was that, another successful cosmic order.

The stylist brought two dresses and a pair of shoes with her! I took the bag off to the ladies to change but - ugghh - not me at all. I was persuaded to wear them but I felt uncomfortable in the dresses and the shoes were far too high for me. As I tottered about I began to feel like Miss Piggy!! It was awful and the photographer had me posing in certain ways that fitted their newspaper style but was so not me. I was unhappy with the whole thing and didn't want the article to appear. Why the bloody hell hadn't I been more specific about the order and emphasised it be a successful photo shoot for the good of ALL concerned?

But there's the lesson - I hurriedly put in a cosmic order but I hadn't thought it through first. I hadn't been specific about what I wanted the outcome to be and I certainly hadn't managed my expectations.

I placed another order that evening and the article never appeared in the paper. Success.

Breast Cancer Support Group

I just want to share this story with you, which is a classic example of the way Spirit works and why sometimes we have to be patient. You already know that I had breast cancer and went through surgery, chemotherapy and radiotherapy and came out the other side. Well I never did anything with that whole experience other than be grateful that I survived, but always felt that something positive should have come from it.

It was sometime during the summer that I received an e-mail from a lady asking me to ask if I would take her through her Reiki Level I training. She lived in Panama and had found the Centre on Google! Wow, long way to come to do Reiki training but, yes, of course I would accept her for training.

Training day came, we met and she was lovely. But I have to say that I trusted Spirit to only bring lovely people to our Centre and they never let me down.

During the lunch break we were just chatting. She was a medic working with the poorer communities in Panama. How refreshing, a medic embracing Reiki! The subject somehow turned to breast cancer and I told her my own story. I added at the end that I didn't know what I should do with the whole experience but felt that it shouldn't be wasted.

She looked at me and just smiled.

"It's simple," she said, "you help other women who are going through the same experience that you did".

She felt I had a wonderful opportunity to do some fabulous work with women going through breast cancer and that she felt sure I would gain the support of the medical profession. Really? It was something that had crossed my mind but I had never done anything about it, simply because I thought I couldn't. We talked for a long time and she offered to help in any way she could.

Spirit had done it again! They needed to get this lady, a trained doctor, all the way from Panama and into the Centre. They needed to get breast cancer into the conversation and they needed to plant the seed. They needed to get me to listen and they even needed to give me a bit of a nudge! Not a simple task, but they did it.

In October of the same year we launched our breast cancer support group.

The group ran for many years but sadly was forced to close during the Covid pandemic.

> *We do not create our destiny; we participate in its unfolding. Synchronicity works as a catalyst toward the working out of that destiny*

David Richo

Some Years Later

Gill and I continued to work away in Como for quite a few years and we learnt many things over that time. It was always a pleasure to learn and teach and we loved nothing better than seeing our students grow as individuals. It was an honour to have been part of their journey.

But times were changing. Little did we know then how those changes would affect us all.

We started to realise that our business was beginning to dwindle, not because of anything that we were doing wrong but because our competition was growing. A whole host of training providers were springing up on-line offering everything that we taught and more. They had something we never had – money! They put into place bigger and better systems to deliver on-line training courses. They attracted students from all over the world and because of the sheer numbers could offer huge discounts. We simply could not compete.

With our expenses continuing to rise but our income declining, we knew we had to do something radical and soon. During one of our afternoon sessions in our beautiful space Gill suggested that we seriously think about giving up our premises. I was gutted, but it made perfect sense as we would soon be struggling to pay the rent. We both thought long and hard but could see no other option so on a sad day in November we made the decision to give up our space. We did agree, however, that Como would continue and that we would just rent space as and when needed.

Now our Angels, Guides, the Universe, etc, certainly knew this was the right thing for us to do and they were helping us all the way. In fact, it was probably their idea in the first place and we just picked up on the energies they sent us. Within 24-hours of us making the decision we had two new spaces lined up and they were both a perfect match for what we did, and our holistic and beauty training would be carried out in our tutors' own salons.

We also knew that by letting the premises go we would have to get rid of all the equipment and furniture we had amassed over the years and sat for ages pondering over who on earth would want our huge gong! We needn't have worried at all because in a few short weeks we managed to sell most of the contents we no longer needed, the rest we gave to charity.

Things were looking up although it was a very tearful day when, just before Christmas, we shut the door for the final time and handed back the keys.

In January 2020, we started working out of the rented premises. No, it wasn't quite the same and both Gill and I missed our own space. But financially we had no choice so we just had to be grateful for the time we had there and move forward. Little did we know at that time what was just around the corner!

Covid struck the world and it was a very frightening time for everyone. We held our regular workshops in March 2020 but agreed at the end of each session that we would take a couple of months break until the whole thing blew over! We didn't know then that that was to be our last time together in the same space as a week later we were in our first lockdown.

We continued for a while via Zoom and we were all optimistic that it would only be for a few months before we could get back together. Sadly, that never happened.

Lockdown finally ended and we could work in groups again, salons and training establishments could re-open and we started advertising our courses. We plodded on for the rest of the year but the lockdown had impacted on the nation in a variety of different ways, and many people had lost their jobs or were living on reduced incomes. There was no extra money and no income for us. Like many we couldn't sustain our business so sadly we were forced to close in 2021.

Now What?

The year the Covid pandemic hit the world was a pivotal year for many. The one thing that we had in abundance was time and for many it was a time of reflection and realising what was important in life and what wasn't. Some of us turned to different things, whether as hobbies or in preparation for new careers.

Gill took a course in candle making and has now turned what started as a hobby into her full-time business. She is happy and delighted with the choice she made.

I, on the other hand, felt totally lost. My beloved Como had gone and I just didn't know what to do with my time, and I didn't know what lie ahead for me. Not a good place for someone who always wanted to know what was next. On top of all that I felt that I had lost my best friend too as we couldn't see each other. Yes, we spoke over Zoom, FaceTime and WhatsApp daily but it's not the same as sitting in the same room with a coffee, or more probably a glass of wine, with your bestie.

Our holidays were all cancelled, so no jetting off to Croatia with Gill and no cruising with Pat. Jordan couldn't come home. I had nothing to look forward to. But I wasn't alone there, it was happening to everyone.

My year got worse when I was diagnosed with breast cancer again in June. Shitting bloody hell, could life get any worse? Well yes, of course it could, at least I was still alive and hadn't caught Covid.

But, if the media was anything to go by, that was just a matter of time!

I kept a journal of how I was dealing with the cancer and recorded my thoughts, feelings and emotions around the whole experience. I also started to use some of the things I had learnt over the years and gradually began to get the old me back. Later that year I decided to turn the journal into a book and so turned to writing. What I discovered during that period was a love of writing which I never knew existed. I worked with a book coach and publisher and my first book, *Once Bitten, Twice Prepared*, was published in April of the following year.

Once I finished writing the book I was back to feeling lost. My mission had been completed, what next. Well next was another book, this one. And after this one I have another in the wings, and with the next one I will turn my hand to fiction.

When one door closes, another one opens

And Now

Here we are, bang up to date. I don't know what will happen next, or where I will be in 5-year's time. And that's ok because I think I've finally learned that I am not in complete control of my life. Yes, I have choices but my life will ebb and flow exactly how it is meant to.

Maybe in 5-year's time I will be a famous author with a string of books under my belt. Or maybe my life will take a different turn altogether. I might even be dead. I hope not, but if I am then I will have gone home. All will be as it should be.

My spiritual journey has been an amazing one, full of insight, clarity and strange happenings. Of course, it didn't just happen overnight, it took years to get to the place where I am now. My journey hasn't finished and never will.

What I have learned over the years is that you don't have to be special to become spiritual. You don't have to go and meditate on top of a mountain, or go into seclusion, or take yourself off to an Ashram to learn spirituality. My son has done all those things on his journey and gained great insight from each of them, but it's not necessary. For me, my life is my practice and I don't feel the need to take myself off. My spiritual life runs alongside my day-to-day life and works perfectly well for me.

But you do need to start somewhere. For me it was a chance visit to a spiritualist church, for you it will be something completely different. Maybe someone you meet, a tv programme, a film or a book you read. Something will trigger you and you'll be off on such a fabulous adventure that never ends.

Acknowledgements

There were so many people involved in my journey and I thank them all. The people who have given me the knowledge I needed at the time to enable me to move forward, and the people who just popped in to help with life lessons.

I thank Brit Lashae and Julia Poor at Journey Written for reading, editing and publishing my book; and to Warren Brown, at Brown Creative Ltd, for another stunning book cover.

I thank the people who have shown up in my life and stayed there – you all know who you are. I am grateful to have three best friends – how did I get to be so lucky?

I thank you, my reader, for reading my story and ask that if you've enjoyed it would you kindly leave a review on Amazon. I would be grateful and I'll probably pop you in my gratitude diary.

But most of all I must thank Junie for her ridiculous idea of going to the Spiritualist Church in the first place. Who knew then where that was going to lead?

Printed in Great Britain
by Amazon

65325467R00116